Walk LEVITICUS!

ויקרא

And He called

Jeffrey Enoch Feinberg, Ph.D.

illustrations by Kim Alan Moudy

Messianic Jewish Publishers
a division of
Messianic Jewish Communications
Baltimore, Maryland

06 05 04 03 02 01 6 5 4 3 2 1

ISBN 1-880226-92-8
Library of Congress Catalog Control Number: 2001088469

Walk Leviticus! belongs to
the UMJC Special Collection
of recommended resources.

Messianic Jewish Publishers
6204 Park Heights Avenue
Baltimore, Maryland 21215
(410) 358-6471

Distributed by
Messianic Jewish Resources International
Individual order line: (800) 410-7367
Trade order line: (800) 733-MJRI (6574)
E-mail: lederer@messianicjewish.net
Website: www.messianicjewish.net

Acknowledgements

Special thanks to Jay, Dan, and Pat.
JEF

Dedicated to those
who follow God's instructions
to walk in holiness.
"I am ADONAI, who sets you apart to be holy."
Leviticus 20:8b

Preface

Leviticus may seem anachronistic to today's readers, who have never known a world that accepts God's manifest Presence as obvious. Modern man does not really expect to hear a sudden news flash that God has returned to the Temple Mount in Jerusalem! Most people have not considered death to be a divine appointment to stand resurrected before the very Throne of God. When one starkly faces the reality and changeability of life, however, the call to holiness becomes central.

Walk Leviticus! spells out the implications of holiness for redeeming life. Imagine a reality in which God actually lives in the camp of Yisra'el! Life is forever altered by this reality. Those in covenant with the living God are now set apart from the nations, to live in a holy camp that radiates with the Presence of God. Moshe enters the Tent of Meeting to hear divine instruction personally spoken by God Himself. Starting with Moshe, God calls the nation to be holy. Holiness must be maintained in the camp; or else God will progressively withdraw His Presence, His blessing, and His protection.

The Tabernacle can now be seen as a miniature Mt. Sinai. The Holy of Holies, enshrouded in a cloud of incense, recalls the ancient memory of the divine cloud at the summit of Sinai, where heaven touched earth. Suddenly the Shavu'ot experience of reliving the covenant with God becomes portable, as God accompanies His people en route to the Land of Promise!

A divine plan for redeeming life emerges. God separates out His people to grow into a holy nation. In the process, man inches back toward Gan Eden, the place where heaven and earth merge into paradise. Leviticus shows how the individual can impact a household, how households can impact communities, and how communities can transform their environments.

As creation is leavened with God's holiness, even the weather patterns, crop yields, and animal kingdom are affected. All life is connected, and living out the blessings of the covenant sets up a spiral in time across generations. Blessings multiply, leading to long life, increased fruitfulness in the land and household, and finally the transformation of avodah (*work*) itself. In fact, the backbreaking conditions of earning a living from an accursed land are replaced by the priestly service of a holy nation. Eventually, life on earth climaxes as avodah (*worship*) in the glorious Presence of the Living God!

A proper understanding of holiness can help every New Covenant priest, clothed in the righteousness of Yeshua, to align his will with God's and co-partner to pray His plan into being. We need to remember that when we're powerless, we should check our holiness barometer. "The effectual fervent prayer of a righteous man availeth much" (James 5:16b, KJV). It is God's holiness that radiates life and transforms the world. We must balance a holy life inside the camp with reaching out to a needy world outside. As New Covenant priests, we must value our access to God and pray for His holiness to change the world.

These are the prayers that understand covenant history from beginning to end. These are the prayers that seek, once again, the manifest Presence of God in the Land, in His holy city, in His holy Temple, among His nation, and among the nations of the world. In this way, all Yisra'el will be saved!

JEF
Sh'mittah, 2000-2001

Walk Leviticus!

Each section begins with a "doodle" of a scene from the portion. Embedded in the scene, cursive Hebrew letters spell out the portion name. Next comes an entertaining synopsis in rhyme. Now on to the meat of the Word! Sub-section titles scope out the flow of the story across the Torah portion, the Haftarah, and related B'rit Chadashah readings. Finally, the phrase at the bottom of the page focuses the reader on the "key idea."

The ***Hiker's Log*** offers a cumulative summary of what has happened to date in the story, a hint at what lies ahead, a box capsulizing the summary, and a second box listing the people, places, and events to come.

For Hebrew lovers, ***Compass Work*** spells out the portion name letter by letter. Scripture supplies the context for this name, and the first verse is analyzed phrase by phrase. Related Words show how the root word gets used in everyday speech.

Starting with the Rishon, each segment of Torah is featured on its own page. The topic verse is quoted, key ideas are emphasized, and challenging discussion questions stimulate contemplation. Please note that the footer at the bottom of each page references the entire segment under discussion. It is recommended that the reader consult the Scripture before reading the commentary for the particular segment.

The name ***Meanderings*** suggests how our journey through Torah now turns to related "excursion side-trips" in the Haftarah (*Prophets*) and B'rit Chadashah (*New Covenant/New Testament*). The format matches that of the Torah sub-sections. Like the maftir, these pages feature a quote from the end of the passage being studied. Due to limited space, ideas are compact. For readers desiring to meditate on these passages, a number of cross-references (cf.) are provided. (***Please note:*** *Selections from the B'rit Chadashah reflect efforts to complement the annual reading cycle for the Torah and Haftarah. It is not suggested that the current selections are the only readings for a given portion.*)

The ***Oasis*** has two segments: *Talk Your Walk,* a conclusion drawn from the portion; and *Walk Your Talk,* a personal application. Remarks in ***Journey's End*** sum up all of Leviticus.

Hebrew names for Torah portions, people, places, and terms of interest are sprinkled throughout the text to add cultural context to the story. The italicized English meaning generally follows in parentheses; otherwise, check the ***Glossary***. Whenever verse numbers vary, the references for the Tanakh are given in parentheses with the Hebrew תנ"ך to identify them.

To use this volume as a daily devotional, the following reading plan is suggested. Begin just after Shabbat to prepare for the next week's reading, typically listed on any Jewish calendar.

Sunday	*Hiker's Log* and *Compass Work* (overview)
Monday	*Rishon* and *Sheni* Sections of the Torah portion
Tuesday	*Shlishi* and *R'vi'i* Sections
Wednesday	*Chamishi* and *Shishi* Sections
Thursday	*Shvi'i* and *Maftir* Sections
Friday	*Meanderings* (Haftarah and B'rit Chadashah)
Saturday	*Oasis* (summary and application)

Readers with less time might browse each chapter as one might page through a magazine. The *Hiker's Log* and *Oasis* segments offer the best overview.

Table of

Contents

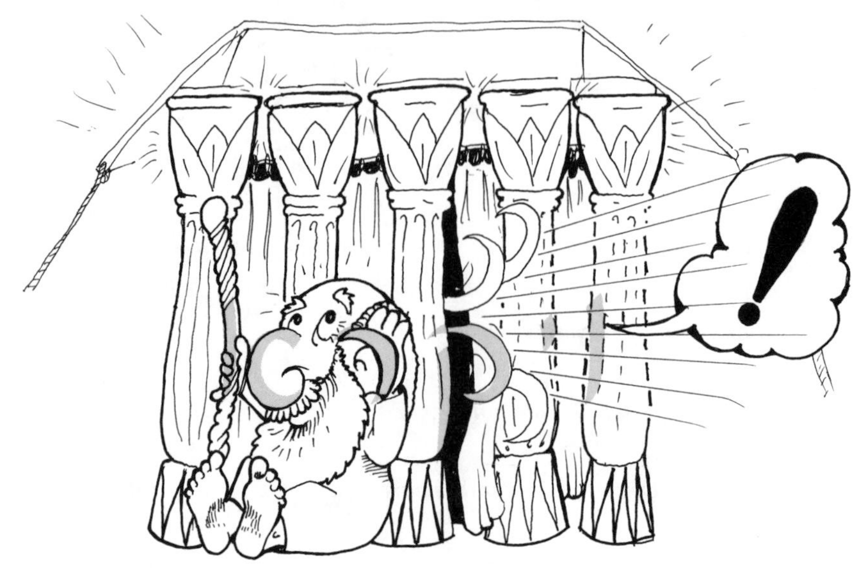

ויקרא!

And God called
Moshe to the Tent.
He said, "Olah
is the smoke of ascent.
Make the whole thing smoke,
make sure it is spent.
Then come to Me humbly,
a wholehearted gent!"

"Bring a tribute of grain
for the priests to eat
and a covenant feast
as the worshippers' treat.
But when you sin,
sprinkle blood near My feet.
To pay for guilt,
you must never cheat!"

Walk VAYIKRA!
1:1-6:7(5:26 תנ"ך)

And He called

TORAH—Leviticus 1:1-6:7(5:26 תנ"ך)

1st God Calls, "Come Near!"—Leviticus 1:1
2nd Ascending to His Presence—Leviticus 1:14
3rd Bringing Tribute—Leviticus 2:7
4th Voluntary Offering—Leviticus 3:1
5th Required Sacrifice—Leviticus 4:1-3
6th Unintended Sin—Leviticus 4:27
7th The Sliding Scale—Leviticus 5:11
Maftir Restitution—Leviticus 6:7 (5:26 תנ"ך)

HAFTARAH—Isaiah 43:21-44:23

Yisra'el Redeemed—Isaiah 44:23

B'RIT CHADASHAH—Hebrews 10:1-18

Sins Removed!—Hebrews 10:18

The Call to Sacrifice

Looking Back

Our Torah study now spans two books. **Sefer B'Reisheet** (*the book of Genesis/in the beginning*) describes the beginnings of the world, mankind, and Avraham's family. This first book concludes as Yisra'el's clan moves to Egypt to survive famine under Yosef's leadership.

Sefer Sh'mot (*the book of Exodus/ these are the names*) continues our story, as God's mighty hand delivers us from slavery and Moshe leads us out. We build God's dwelling and unite as a nation, called to bring all nations to covenant with the God of Avraham, Yitzchak, and Ya'akov.

We now proceed to the third book, **Sefer vaYikra** (*the book of Leviticus/and He called*). Leviticus begins by connecting the story line to the close of Exodus, where we saw that Moshe could not come into the Tent of Meeting because of the Lord's glory (Ex. 40:35). Now, Adonai calls Moshe to enter His Presence.

***B'Reisheet**, in the beginning,*
God creates Paradise,
but we fail to rest.
God begins again with Avraham
and his family of covenant faith.

*And these are the **Sh'mot**, names,*
of the children of Yisra'el
who go down to Egypt
to survive the famine.
As our numbers grow,
we are enslaved.
But God delivers us from bondage
and forms us into a nation!

***vaYikra**—and He calls us*
to become holy for Him!

Many consider Leviticus a technical and difficult book. Yet a five-year-old traditionally begins his study with this book! The call to the priesthood is the child's first exposure to Jewish education. The Midrash quotes God as saying, "Since the children are pure, and the sacrifices are pure let the pure come and occupy themselves with things that are pure" [Lev. R. vii. 3] The call to enter God's Presence characterizes the entire book.

The starting point of Leviticus is a nation in fellowship. Thus, the text moves from (1) the olah (*ascent offering*), an offering given entirely to the LORD; (2) to the minchah (*tribute offering*), a gift or tribute shared by the worshipper with both the LORD and the priests; (3) to the zevach sh'lamim (*fellowship offering*), a covenant feast eaten by all—the worshippers, the priests, and the LORD. This covenant feast reenacts the theophany at Sinai, where the leaders of the nation follow the priests on the path to the clouded summit. Washed clean and ritually purified, seventy elders feast under the feet of the living God . . .

In VAYIKRA . . .

The Key People are Moshe (*Moses*), b'nei Yisra'el (*the children of Israel*), and Aharon's (*Aaron's*) sons—the priests.

The Scene is the tabernacle, in the wilderness of Sinai.

Main Events include the LORD calling to Moshe and giving instructions for bringing the various types of offerings—burnt, grain, peace, sin, and trespass; and more instruction about what the priests will do and what can be eaten.

The Trail Ahead

The Path

	א	רָ	קְ	יִ	וַ
letter:	alef	reish	koof	yod	vav
sound:	(silent)	**Rah**	K'	Yyee	Vah

and He called = VAYIKRA = **ויקרא**

The Legend

and called	*vayikra*	וַיִּקְרָא
to Moses	*el-Moshe*	אֶל־מֹשֶׁה
and spoke the LORD	*va-y'daber ADONAI*	וַיְדַבֵּר יְהֹוָה
to him	*elav*	אֵלָיו
from Tent of Meeting	*me-ohel mo'ed*	מֵאֹהֶל מוֹעֵד
to say . . .	*lemor*	לֵאמֹר:

—*Leviticus 1:1*

Related Words

read, call, name, recite, summon	*kara*	קָרָא
call the roll	*kara et ha-shemote*	קָרָא אֶת הַשֵּׁמוֹת
reading of Scriptures in synagogue	*k'riat ha-Torah*	קְרִיאַת הַתּוֹרָה
holy convocation to proclaim holiness	*mikra-kodesh*	מִקְרָא־קֹדֶשׁ
how do they call you? (i.e. what's your name?)	*eich kor'im l'cha?*	אֵיךְ קוֹרְאִים לְךָ?

Hit the Trail!

God Calls, "Come Near!"

> ***"*** ***ADONAI called to Moshe and spoke to him from the tent of meeting. He said . . . "***
>
> ***—Leviticus 1:1***

Written with a small alef, the word "VAYIKRA" (*and He called!*) hints at the still small voice of the One who calls. Each of us is called to draw near to God, starting with Moshe in verse one.

Called to ascend and face God!

Moshe enters the Ohel Mo'ed (*Tent of Meeting*), where God instructs him on ways the people can approach Him. The olah (*ascent offering*) must be (1) presented at the door of the Tent, (2) assigned as a sacred offering by s'michah (*laying on of hands*), (3) slaughtered, and finally (4) smoked. Flames and smoke of the olah "ascend" heavenward to God.

The common people meet with God in the courtyard, in front of the altar of burnt offerings. Kohanim (*priests*) come closer, to the holy place within, to render priestly service. God calls Moshe, the nation's most humble representative, to come closer still. As at Mt. Sinai, Moshe must enter the glory of God's Presence. Our goal, too.

? ***Today, we take lightly the privilege of entering into the glorious Presence of God. Read Lev. 1:3-9. Detail the steps in the ritual procedure for offering an olah. Explain how these steps can help to inform your prayer life.***

Ascending to His Presence

❝ If his offering to ADONAI is a burnt offering of birds, he must offer a dove or a young pigeon. ❞
—Leviticus 1:14

The olah (*ascent*, or *burnt offering*)—whether cattle, sheep, goat, or in the case of the poor, a tor (*turtledove*) or pigeon—"ascends" in flames to God in heaven. Only the hide remains. The whole animal "ascends" in smoke as rei ach nicho ach (*a sweet savor*), pleasing to God.

The olah "ascends," preparing the way to stand before God!

Presenting an olah assumes the offerer is already in living, covenant relationship with God. The burnt offering atones for sinful thoughts and ideas that have not become deeds. Everyone who ascends to Y'rushalayim for a pilgrimage festival, or who wishes to raise his spiritual level, brings an olah to God's altar [Stone, p. 545, n3].

The purpose of the olah is "to secure an initial response from God" that His worshippers desire "to bring their needs to His attention" [Levine, p. 5]. God looks upon the clean heart and holy intention of the worshipper when He accepts the olah as rei ach nicho ach (*a sweet savor*).

? *Commenting on Hosea 6:6, Carson [p. 96] observes that sacrifice is incompatible with an attitude of "mercilessly nursing enmity, bitterness, or animosity." What attitude makes offering sacrifice compatible with receiving mercy?*

Bringing Tribute

> *" If your offering is a grain offering cooked in a pot, it is to consist of fine flour with olive oil. "*
> *—Leviticus 2:7*

The minchah (*tribute, meal offering*) consists of solet (*semolina*), the finest flour taken solely from the inner kernels. The minchah includes salt which preserves (Lev. 2:13), but not honey or lemon which ferments (Lev. 2:11). As with the olah, God accepts the minchah as reiach nichoach (*a sweet savor*) when offered wholeheartedly.

The priest receives the minchah from the offerer at the door to the Tent of Meeting. Using his three mid-fingers, he scoops out a handful of the meal and smokes it as an azkarah (*reminder portion*).

Bring tribute as holy gifts for God and His priests!

God remits back the rest, called kodesh kodashim (*especially holy part*), to be eaten and enjoyed by Aharon and his sons, in the LORD's Presence, in the holy place of the sanctuary. The minchah affirms the covenant and recalls the memory of the ascent of Aharon and his sons up Mt. Sinai (Ex. 24:1, 8-11).

? *Read Lev. 2:14-16. Note that firstfruits are not "fruits." Minchat bikkurim or "the tribute of first-processed" describes the best of the spring cereal crop. What added ingredients are mixed in the minchat bikkurim besides salt?*

Voluntary Offering

> ***"** If his offering is a sacrifice of peace offerings, then, if he offers before ADONAI an animal from the herd, then, no matter whether it is male or female, it must be without defect.**"** —Leviticus 3:1*

Zevach sh'lamim (*wholeness sacrifice* or *peace offering*) includes the same domesticated cud-chewing herbivores as the olah. Sh'lamim are shared by God, priests, and worshippers at a festive, covenant meal.

As with the olah, God instructs the worshipper to offer the animal at the door of the Tent, to lay hands on the head, and to slaughter the sacrifice. Eating sh'lamim recalls to memory the time when the seventy elders ate and drank upon Sinai in the Presence of the LORD (Ex. 24:9-11).

To prepare for the feast, the priest splashes dam (*blood*), carrier of the animal's life, on the sides of the altar. He smokes the pader (*suet, fat*), covering vital organs where the soul resides, as a reiach nichoach (*sweet savor*) to God (Lev. 3:11). Then he reserves the breast and right thigh for the priests. The worshipper eats what remains at a joyous covenant feast before God and the priests!

Bring fellowship sacrifices for all to feast in the Presence of God!

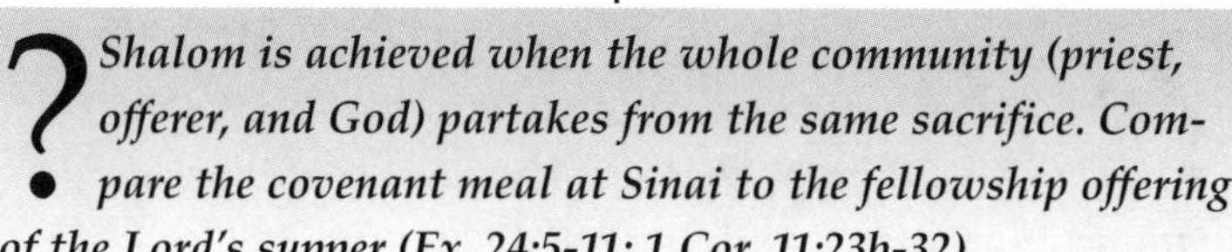

***?** Shalom is achieved when the whole community (priest, offerer, and God) partakes from the same sacrifice. Compare the covenant meal at Sinai to the fellowship offering of the Lord's supper (Ex. 24:5-11; 1 Cor. 11:23b-32).*

Required Sacrifice

" ***Adonai said to Moshe, "Tell the people of Isra'el: 'If anyone sins inadvertently against any of the mitzvot of Adonai . . . he is to offer Adonai a young bull . . . '"***
—Leviticus 4:1-3

Chatta't (*the purification offering*) removes the defilement arising from sin. Sin literally pollutes a place (Lev. 18:24-30), and guilt rests on the area (Dt. 21:1-9). If sin isn't purified, it builds up. Ultimately, it can drive God from living among His people.

A chatta't is required to avoid karet (*cutting off*). In the case of leaders (but not the anointed priest), blood is smeared outside the holy place, on the horns of the outer altar, the altar for burnt offerings. For more serious sins such as sins of the anointed priest or the congregation, blood is smeared inside the holy place, on the horns of the inner altar, the altar of incense (Lev. 4:7, 18, 25). This ritual procedure purifies the place where God dwells.

Life from the soul of a fit sacrifice can restore those who are cut off.

In the New Covenant, the worshipper—not the place—is purified (Eph. 2:13, 22). Holiness is the basic requirement for maintaining the Lord's Presence in the life of the New Covenant priest.

? The western mind does not easily understand the biblical idea that sin is a kind of radioactive pollution that repels God (Gen. 4:10). How, then, can confession decontaminate impurities that drive God away (1 Jn. 1:9)?

Unintended Sin

“If an individual among the people commits a sin inadvertently, doing something against any of the mitzvot of ADONAI concerning things which should not be done, he is guilty.” —*Leviticus 4:27*

Purification offerings are required for individuals who sin, even unintentionally. Sins of omission are described in Lev. 5:1-6. Wenham [p. 93] indicates that forgetting, a “memory slip,” incurs guilt. A person who bears sin is guilty, regardless of whether or not he knows it.

Unintentional sin does not excuse the one who sins.

In general, the more serious the sin, the greater the cost of the sacrifice. Individuals offer small, female goats or ewe lambs for unintended sins (Lev. 4:27-28, 32). The anointed priest or congregation offers a male bull, the largest and most costly of offerings.

The ritual procedure calls for s'micha (*laying on of hands*), which identifies the offerer with the sacrifice. Following s'micha, the offerer slaughters his animal. Then the priest sprinkles the blood on the horns of the outer altar, even in the case of a nasi (*leader*) (Lev. 4:30).

For more serious sins, blood from the chatta't must be applied to the horns of the inner altar (Lev. 4:7, 18).

? ***Read Lev. 4:27-28; 5:1, 3-4. Explain why purification offerings do not atone for intentional sins. Discuss the implication that intentional sins pile up on the horns of the outer and inner altar. What can be done?***

The Sliding Scale

"But if his means are insufficient even for two doves or two young pigeons, then he is to bring as his offering for the sin he committed two quarts of fine flour for a sin offering . . . " —Leviticus 5:11

Provisions for the poor make certain that every person can bring obligatory purification offerings. As with the olah, there is a sliding scale based on what one can truly afford (Lev. 5:7-10).

Costs for purification can be reduced, based on one's ability to pay.

The poorest of all persons can bring an issaron (*one-tenth* ephah of flour; also called an "omer," a day's provision of flour, or two quarts). Everyone must give according to his or her means.

The destitute person who cannot even afford a pair of common pigeons can bring a bloodless chatta't (*purification offering*). The priest treats this chatta't as he would a minchah, scooping and smoking an azkarah (*reminder*) at the outer altar as an isheh (*fire offering*) to the LORD (Lev. 5:12-13). It is striking that the priest can make atonement at the outer altar with a bloodless sacrifice. But a wealthy person, bringing the same omer of flour, would incur guilt for entering the courtyard with an unsanctified offering [Ker. 28a].

? The offering for a person without adequate means is called a korban oleh v'yored (near-offering, up and down). Study Lev. 5:11. What ingredients are excluded? How can a bloodless offering atone for the poor?

Restitution

> *“Thus the cohen will make atonement for him before* ADONAI, *and he will be forgiven in regard to whatever it was he did that made him guilty.”*
>
> *—Leviticus 6:7 (5:26 תנ״ך)*

Only the asham (*guilt or reparation offering*) atones for stealing holy property or falsely swearing by God's name in court. Using God's name or property to gain personal advantage incurs guilt. Such ma'alah ma'al (*breach of faith*) violates the third commandment (Ex. 20:7).

To avert punishment, the person must seek reconciliation (Lev. 6:2-5 (5:21-24 תנ״ך)). Forgiveness alone is not sufficient! The guilty must take practical, economic steps to settle with the victim [Bava Kamma 110a; Mt. 5:23-26].

Restitution requires the return of stolen goods and an additional twenty percent (considered a light penalty). The guilty party then offers a two-year-old ram that is tam (*whole, unblemished*), "by your assessment in silver . . . as an asham" (Fox, Lev. 5:15, 25).

The price for guilt incurred cannot be reduced!

Torah classifies six types of reparation offerings, and in each instance requires a blood sacrifice that is not subject to reduction in kind or in cost.

? ***Read Luke 19:8-9. Describe Zacchaeus's attitude toward restitution. Read Exodus 21:37 (22:1 תנ״ך). Comment on the large fines for stealing and selling livestock, and contrast this with the restitution required for stealing from God.***

Yisra'el Redeemed *Meander*

" Sing, you heavens, for ADONAI has done it! Shout, you depths of the earth! . . . For ADONAI has redeemed Ya'akov; he glorifies himself in Isra'el. "

—Isaiah 44:23

In this week's haftarah reading, Y'rushalayim has been destroyed. It is no longer possible to bring offerings to the altar of God's dwelling. Addressing the exiles, Isaiah explains that God has been weighed down by the sins of the people and by offerings which are not heartfelt (Is. 43:23-24).

So now, God announces a new way—He will wipe away sins for His glory alone (Is. 43:25). He will judge offerings given with wholeness of heart as acceptable to Him. "I wipe away your offenses," God tells Yisra'el (Is. 44:22a). The nation will yet fulfill its calling to glorify the LORD.

Yisra'el is still called to draw near to God!

Echoing the words of Isaiah 43:10, the LORD raises up Yisra'el to be His witness. Worshippers from idolatrous nations (Is. 44:9) become as blind and unthinking as the wood from their carved idols. But Yisra'el will break out in song—its forests and trees alive, its people redeemed and glorified!

? *The purpose of offerings has always been to maintain the covenant relationship. Abuses led to the defiling of the Temple and God's resulting departure. Read Romans 11:25-27. What sin does God promise to remove from Yisra'el?*

Sins Removed!

“Now where there is forgiveness for these, an offering for sins is no longer needed.”

—Hebrews 10:18

In this reading, the author of Hebrews quotes the judgment of Isaiah concerning the abuses of sin, meal, and burnt offerings. Then quoting the Psalms, he adds, ". . . you have prepared for me a body . . . I have come to do your will" (Heb. 10:5-7). Messiah cleanses our very bodies, to form a suitable dwelling place for God!

By sacrificing His life, shedding His blood as an asham (*reparation*) (Is. 53:10), Messiah cleanses the hearts and purges the consciences of those who believe (Heb. 10:2). Scripture announces a new way to approach God in holiness (Heb. 10:9-10), the perfecting (or making whole) of those who are now being sanctified (Heb. 10:14).

Messiah has paid the full price for our guilt!

God's promise not to remember sins presupposes a putting away or afesis (Greek word meaning *removal*). Forgiveness means the complete removal of sins, making future purification offerings for sin unnecessary (Heb. 10:17-18).

? *Lev. 5:17-19 describes the asham talu'i (the doubtful reparation offering), required whenever a person wonders about unknowingly violating a prohibition. Explain how Messiah's death purges our conscience from guilt.*

Talk Your Walk . . .

VAYIKRA ADONAI (*and the LORD called*) a nation of redeemed firstborns to the priesthood during the great moment when His Spirit flooded the tabernacle. First, God calls Moshe to enter the Tent of Meeting alone. The LORD speaks to Moshe directly about sacrifices His people must bring, as they draw near to serve the living God.

In-communion offerings include the olah, the minchah, and the sh'lamim. God prescribes the <u>olah</u>, as a dedication of the whole person to holy service. The entire olah ascends to heaven in smoke. The offering is prepared for the altar, its skin going to the officiating priest, its fat smoked as reiach nichoach (*a sweet savor*) to the LORD, and its entrails to the dung heap outside the city. The olah is burnt in its entirety on the copper altar, outside the Tent. The <u>minchah</u> is prescribed as a tribute paid to God (and food for the priests), and the <u>sh'lamim</u> (*fellowship offerings*) as a festivity for worshipper, priest, and God together.

Rules of holiness govern our approach to God.

Out-of-communion offerings restore the relationship between the worshipper and God. These include the chatta't and asham. The <u>chatta't</u>, or purification offering, purifies or de-sins the individual. The <u>asham</u>, or reparation, requires wholehearted repentance and restitution. The community's sins require sprinkling at the inner altar or, on Yom Kippur, at God's feet!

Oasis

. . . Walk Your Talk

Are you prepared to offer yourself as an olah (*ascent offering*) for the LORD? Says Romans, "I exhort you . . . to offer yourselves as a sacrifice, living and set apart for God . . . the logical 'Temple worship' for you" (Ro. 12:1). Those who devote their whole lives to the service of bringing glory to God become as a sweet savor that ascends in pure and wholehearted relationship with God. This "smoke" transcends the constraints of the body, and it allows the pure in heart to ascend ("aliyah," *go up*) to God.

The victims of the Holocaust saw only terror at the camps. The world was silent as their smoke and ashes ascended the chimneys of the extermination camps. No one can fathom the loss of six million (or twelve million, if you count the castoffs and Christians). Was God silent in the face of the world's silence?

God treasures the "sweet savor" of those who draw near!

A conscience-stricken world voted the nation of Yisra'el into being. Am Yisra'el chai (*the people of Israel live*)—through their children and their children's children! You can choose, spiritually, to offer yourself as an olah for God. But are you willing to give Him your whole self? Will your ashes be His glory?

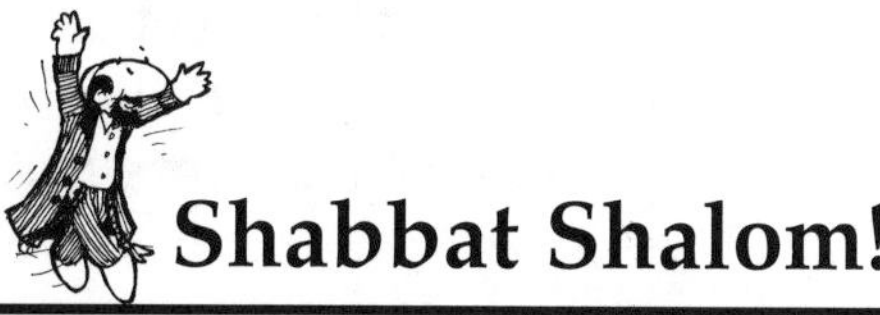

צו!

It's the time
of the great command
when Aaron is ordained
High Priest of the land!
The eating of blood and fat
is banned.
And Moshe obeys,
just as God planned!

He offers a bullock
for the sins of the priests,
smears the altar's horns
with the blood of beasts.
So the sanctuary's clean
for the covenant feasts.
One week with God,
then the priests are released!

Walk Tsav!
6:8(1 תנ״ך)-8:36

Command!

Torah—Leviticus 6:8(1 תנ״ך)-8:36

- 1st Command the Kohanim!—Leviticus 6:8-9(1-2 תנ״ך)
- 2nd The Kohen's Offerings—Leviticus 6:19-20a(12-13a תנ״ך)
- 3rd The Kohen's Thanksgiving—Leviticus 7:11
- 4th Consecrating the Kohanim—Leviticus 8:1-3
- 5th The Kohen's Purification—Leviticus 8:14
- 6th The Kohen's Consecration—Leviticus 8:22
- 7th The Kohen's Elevation—Leviticus 8:30
- Maftir The Command Completed!—Leviticus 8:36

Haftarah—Jeremiah 7:21-8:3; 9:23-24(22-23 תנ״ך)

Reflect Glory—Jeremiah 9:24(23 תנ״ך)

B'rit Chadashah—Hebrews 9:11-28

Face to Face—Hebrews 9:28

The Command
for Priestly Service

Looking Back

B'REISHEET (*in the beginning*), God created man to rule creation. When we disobeyed, God banned us from paradise, but continued to work with individuals. He raised up patriarchs and then a royal family.

These are **SH'MOT** (*names*) of the sons of Yisra'el, chosen to be a priestly nation to reach the nations of the world. God covenants to dwell in the midst of this nation.

VAYIKRA ADONAI (*and the LORD called*) to Moshe, and then every Israelite, to be holy and come close, bringing offerings.

ADONAI tells Moshe, **TSAV** et-Aharon (*command Aaron!*) and his sons regarding their priestly role in sacrificial rituals.

The portion opens with commands concerning priestly instruction for receiving offerings: (1) the olah (*ascent offering*); (2) the minchah (*meal offering*) as tribute for priests; (3) the sin or purification offerings and guilt or reparation offerings, for those who are out-of-the camp or out-of-communion with God; and finally, (4) sh'lamim (*fellowship offerings*), which are eaten festively by all.

VAYIKRA ***ADONAI,***
and the Lord called us,
to come into the Tent and
be holy for Him.
But how can we approach?

It is the LORD who leads the way.
He instructs Moshe, "TSAV—
command the priests! . . . "
Once Moshe consecrates
and sanctifies them,
with zeal
they enter into
His Holy Presence.

Thereafter, both the tabernacle and kohanim (*priests*) are anointed for the priestly service of the nation.

Log

Five portions spanning Exodus and Leviticus, from **T'TSAVEH** (*you shall command*) to **TSAV** (*command!*), link together into a meaningful whole, which ties the calling of the nation to the activities of the priesthood.

With detailed instructions, the LORD directs Moshe: **T'TSAVEH** (*you shall command*) the consecration and ordination of the priests (Ex. 29). **KI TISA** (*when you elevate*) the nation, it can reach the state of being in-communion with God. **VAYAKHEL** Moshe (*Moses assembles*) the people to make God's dwelling. **P'KUDEI** (*accounts of*) materials used are summarized, and God fills the dwelling with His Presence.

VAYIKRA ADONAI (*and the* LORD *called*) the people to bring sacrifices. God tells Moshe: **TSAV** (*command!*) the priests to receive offerings from the children of Yisra'el; to maintain purity in the mishkan (*dwelling*); and to follow the LORD's command to draw near to Him on behalf of the people with purity and fullness of heart . . .

In TSAV . . .

The Key People are Moshe (*Moses*), Aharon (*Aaron*), and Aharon's sons.

The Scene is the wilderness of Sinai.

The Main Events include the Lord's instructions for the burnt offering, grain offering, sin offering, trespass offering, and peace offerings; dressing Aharon and his sons in priestly garments, anointing the tabernacle, and consecrating all that is in it; the seven-day period while the priests remain inside the tabernacle; and Aharon and sons doing all the LORD has commanded by the hand of Moshe.

The Trail Ahead 

The Path

	ו	צַ
letter:	vav	tsadee
sound:	V	**TSah**

command! = **TSAV** = **צו**

The Legend

and spoke the Lord	*va-y'da**ber** ADONAI*	וַיְדַבֵּר יְהוָה
to Moses to say	*el-Mo**she** le**mor***	אֶל־מֹשֶׁה לֵּאמֹר׃
<u>command</u> — Aaron	*<u>**tsav**</u> et-Aha**ron***	צַו אֶת־אַהֲרֹן
and — sons-his to say	*v'et-ba**nav** le**mor***	וְאֶת־בָּנָיו לֵאמֹר
this (is) instruction of the burnt offering	*zot to**rat** ha-o**lah***	זֹאת תּוֹרַת הָעֹלָה
she/it the burnt offering	*hee ha-o**lah***	הִוא הָעֹלָה
on the hearth	*al mok**dah***	עַל מוֹקְדָה
on the altar	*al-ha-miz'**be**-ach*	עַל־הַמִּזְבֵּחַ
all the night	*kol-ha-**lai**lah*	כָּל־הַלַּיְלָה
til the morning	*ad-ha-**bo**ker*	עַד־הַבֹּקֶר
and fire of the altar	*v'**esh** ha-miz'**be**-ach*	וְאֵשׁ הַמִּזְבֵּחַ
will be kept burning in him	***too**kad bo*	תּוּקַד בּוֹ׃

—*Leviticus 6:8-9a*(1-2a תנ״ך)

Related Words

you will command (Ex. 27:20)	*t'tsa**veh***	תְּצַוֶּה
command, good deed, religious duty	*mits**vah***	מִצְוָה
son of the commandment	*bar mitz**vah***	בַּר־מִצְוָה
daughter of the commandment	*bat mitz**vah***	בַּת־מִצְוָה
commander, governor	*m'tsa**veh***	מְצַוֶּה
command, order, imperative	*tsi**vooi***	צִוּוּי
will, testament	*tsavva'**ah***	צַוָּאָה

Hit the Trail!

Command the Kohanim!

“ . . . “Give this order to Aharon and his sons: ‘This is the law for the burnt offering [‘olah]: it is what goes up . . . all night long . . . in this way the fire of the altar will be kept burning.’” ”—Lev. 6:8-9(1-2 תנ״ך)

Commands issued to Aharon and sons spell out priestly duties for receiving offerings and sacrifices brought by the people. Stated as an imperative, the LORD orders Moshe, **TSAV** (*command!*) Aharon and sons to be zealous to serve God.

The LORD commands the priests concerning rituals.

The previous portion directed worshippers to bring the right offering for the right occasion. Here, the priests receive additional detailed instructions for correctly receiving the sacrifices which worshippers bring [Ramban].

This is the torat (*instruction of*) the olah (Lev. 6:8-13(1-6תנ״ך)), the minchah (Lev. 6:14-18(7-11תנ״ך)), the chatta't (Lev. 6:24-30(17-23תנ״ך)), the asham (Lev. 7:1-10), and the sh'lamim (Lev. 7:11-21). The order of sacrifices contrasts with the order (from in-communion offerings to out-of-communion offerings) prescribed to the laity in the previous portion (see review on page 26).

***?** This portion, directed to the priests, classifies sacrifices from most to least frequent. Explain why priests would be more interested in the order of frequency of sacrifices than in the order listed in the previous portion for the laity.*

The Kohen's Offerings

***"* Adonai *said to Moshe, "This is the offering for* Adonai *that Aharon and his sons are to offer on the day he is anointed: two quarts of fine flour . . . as a grain offering . . . "* —*Leviticus 6:19-20a* (12-13*a* תנ"ך)**

Additional laws for the offerings reveal the principle that kohanim benefit only from services performed on behalf of others.

First, however, the text requires the priest, upon approaching his Sovereign at the Tent of Meeting for the first time, to bring a minchah [Men. 78a, cf. Ya'akov's *tribute* to Esav in Gen. 32:3].

Additionally, the Kohen Gadol (*High Priest*) brings a minchah on the day of his installation. As representative of the nation, the Kohen Gadol commences every day with an olat tamid (*daily offering*) accompanied by a minchah (Lev. 6:13). No other sacrifice can be accepted on the altar until the olat tamid is offered [Tem. 3:18].

***First, offer tribute to the* Lord.**

Thereafter, the kohen who performs the sacrificial service on behalf of others receives his share, whether from the remainder of the minchah for the nation or from the kodesh kodashim (*holy of holies*) of the chatta't or asham (Lev. 6:9-10).

? ***Explain why the offerings of individuals could not be presented to the* Lord *until the Kohen Gadol had first presented a minchah (tribute) on behalf of the nation. Why would the national offering have to come first?***

The Kohen's Thanksgiving

❝ This is the law for sacrificing peace offerings offered to Adonai . . . ❞

—Leviticus 7:11

Sh'lamim (*fellowship offerings*) include the todah (*thank offering*). Some sh'lamim, such as the neder (*vow*) and the n'davah (*free will*) offerings, must be eaten in two days. Most interestingly, the todah (*thanksgiving*) must be eaten in one day.

Celebrate God's miracles by eating the todah and glorifying God.

The Midrash says that there will always be thank offerings, but that after the coming of Messiah and the perfection of the world, all offerings will be abolished except for the thanksgiving offering [Lev. R. 9:2, 7]. The todah expresses the importance of giving gratitude to God. Indeed, there is a teaching that in messianic times, people will bless God for what appears to be bad, because they will realize that everything God does is ultimately for the good [Pes. 50a; Ro. 8:28]. Note that the todah is brought by one who has survived a life threatening crisis, whether in the desert, in prison, from illness, or at sea (Ps. 107:21-22, cf. 2 Cor. 11:22-31, 13:4).

? *Read Lev. 7:12-13, 20. Forty loaves accompany the todah [Men. 77a], a festivity where the worshipper tells of miracles and thanks God for well-being (Ps. 116:17-19). How do Passover and the Lord's Supper describe a todah festivity?*

Consecrating the Kohanim

> ***“** Adonai said to Moshe, “Take Aharon and his sons with him, the garments, the anointing oil, . . . and assemble the entire community at the entrance to the tent of meeting.” **”*** *—Leviticus 8:1-3*

Ordination proceeds, linking T’TSAVEH (*you shall command*, Ex. 29:1-37) to TSAV (*command!*, Lev. 6:8(1 תנ״ך)-8:36). With exacting obedience, Moshe brings Aharon and his four sons to the laver, and he washes them with water. He dresses Aharon in the standard clothing of priests: tunic, sash, robe, and ephod. Upon Aharon alone, Moshe places the ornate garb of Kohen Gadol (*High Priest*), including the breastplate with Urim and Thummim, the turban, and the golden plate inscribed “Holy to ADONAI.” He anoints both Aharon and the tabernacle with oil, sanctifying them as sacred vessels, set apart for the LORD.

Moshe ordains Aharon and his sons as priests.

In all aspects of priestly service, attention to exacting detail is scrupulous, ka’asher tsivah ADONAI et Moshe (*just as the LORD commanded Moshe*) [note Lev. 7:36, 38, 8:4, 5, 9, 13, 17, 21, 29, 34, 35; cf. *Walk Exodus!*, pp.145, 198]. To complete the holy tasks of God requires complete obedience.

? On Mount Sinai, God instructs Moshe to ordain the priesthood. Ordination of the priests follows building the tabernacle and instructions for receiving sacrifices from the people. Relate Torah to praxis (instruction by doing).

The Kohen's Purification

"Then the young bull for the sin offering was brought, and Aharon and his sons laid their hands on the head of the bull for the sin offering."
—Leviticus 8:14

Kohanim must be anointed (Lev. 8:12), purified (Lev. 8:14), consecrated (Lev. 8:22), and sanctified (Lev. 8:30) to enter into holy service. But first of all, the altar must be prepared.

Priests purify the altar's extremities for service.

Moshe offers the bull of chatta't (*purification*) to sanctify the outer altar [Ex. 29:43; *Walk Exodus!*, p. 147]. Temporarily acting as Kohen Gadol, he decontaminates the altar by applying blood to the horns—the altar's extremities (Lev. 8:15). Fat and entrails are "turned-to-smoke" as God's portion, while the rest of the bull (skin, flesh, and dung) is burned outside the camp (Lev. 8:16-17).

Now the process of setting apart a holy priesthood may begin. The ram of olah (*ascent*) purifies the priests for wholehearted service. Following s'michah (*laying on of hands*), the priest slaughters, sprinkles, sections, and then smokes the ram, outside on the altar of ascent offerings (Lev. 8:19-20). Ordaining the priesthood elevates the nation to serve the LORD.

? *Ordination lasts a week, from the 23rd of Adar to the 1st of Nisan [Stone, p. 588]. During this week, kohanim remain at the tabernacle. In what ways are we as New Covenant priests set apart today to draw near to God?*

The Kohen's Consecration

"Then the other ram was presented, the ram of consecration; Aharon and his sons laid their hands on the head of the ram."

—Leviticus 8:22

The second ram, eyl ha-miluim (*the ram of filling of hands*, also called the *ram of installation*), is presented [Fox, p. 541]. Moshe slaughters this ram. Then he applies the blood of the ram to Aharon's right ear, the thumb of his right hand, and the great toe of his right foot—that Aharon might be wholly devoted to hearing God, to doing the service of the tabernacle, and to walking humbly before the LORD.

The right thigh of the eyl ha-miluim, ordinarily reserved as the priestly portion, is elevated and "turned-to-smoke," so that the priests do not benefit from a sacrifice offered on their behalf.

Priests purify their own extremities for service.

However, the chazeh (*breast*) is lifted up as a t'nufah (*elevation offering*) and given to Moshe, as the portion reserved for the Kohen Gadol (Lev. 8:29). God and Moshe partner to fill the duties of Aharon prior to his official installation [Wenham, p. 142].

? *Read Judges 17:5, 12. Perhaps you have been ordained for service as a leader, elder, shammash, children's worker, musician, or usher. Has God "filled your hands" to serve Him? Explain the role of wholehearted service in ministry.*

The Kohen's Elevation

"Moshe took some of the anointing oil and some of the blood . . . and sprinkled it on Aharon . . . and consecrated Aharon and his clothing together with his sons and their clothing."* —*Leviticus 8:30

Dashing the blood from the ram of ordination upon the altar, Moshe then gathers some of the blood, mixes it with anointing oil, and sprinkles it on the priests and their garments to sanctify them (Lev. 8:24).

Ordination, or "filling the hands," takes seven days.

Thereafter, Aharon and his sons eat the meat of this most sacred sh'lamim (*fellowship offering*) in the sacred inner courtyard of the tabernacle between the altar and door. What is not eaten is destroyed in the morning, so that nothing is eaten from the sacrifice on the third day (Lev. 7:17).

This sacrificial meal of thanksgiving is repeated for seven days as the hands of the anointed are filled [Sifra]. The priests eat matzah from the basket of ordination along with meat from the eyl ha-miluim (*ram of filling/ordination*) (Lev. 8:32, cf. Lev. 6:12-16). The installation ceremony requires seven days for the kohanim to be filled with power. Being elevated for divine service requires a Shabbat with God!

***?** Review Ex. 24:3-8. Sprinkling people and clothing with the blood of fellowship offerings seals a covenant, elevating them for service. Who is elevated for service at Sinai, and who is elevated for service in the above ceremony?*

The Command Completed!

"** Aharon and his sons did all the things which ADONAI ordered through Moshe.* **"

—Leviticus 8:36

Aharon and sons enter an elaborate ritual designed to sanctify them for priestly service. God first outlined this plan when He told Moshe, "T'TSAVEH (*you shall command*)" (Ex. 29:35). Now God sets His plan in motion, saying, "TSAV (*command!*)" (Lev. 6:8-9(1-2ך"תנ)).

Aharon and his sons wait seven days to become holy.

Moshe commands the priests to remain for seven days—"for so I have been commanded" (Lev. 8:35). The priests then abide in the zone of holiness without interruption. Remaining within the sacred courtyard, they absorb holiness by divine command.

Plaut [p. 622] refers to this infusion of godly holiness as "a rising trilogy," anoint, inaugurate, and consecrate—literally, *you shall anoint . . . fill hands . . . make holy, and they shall 'kohen' Me* (Ex. 28:41).

Thus, the priests obey the command, exactly as the LORD commanded Moshe (cf. *Walk Exodus!*, pp. 200-201). God's holiness radiates upon the kohanim. Command completed, priests sanctified, the eighth day begins!

***?** Have you ever been set aside for special service to the LORD? Perhaps you were called to fast or to pray for a person. Describe how you waited, holy to the LORD. How did this experience fulfill you?*

Reflect Glory  *Meander*

> ❝ . . . *instead, let the boaster boast about this: that he understands and knows me—that I am* ADONAI, *practicing grace, justice and righteousness in the land . . .* ❞
>
> —*Jeremiah 9:24*(23 תנ"ך)

Sacrifices alone will not please God. But Yisra'el thought, "The Temple, the Temple will protect us!" They did not believe God would let His holy Temple be destroyed.

The prophet calls, but the people fail to respond.

Yirm'yahu (*Jeremiah*) utters the shocking command, "Eat the olah!" (Jer. 7:21. The prophet decries the people for "burning their sons and daughters in fire—which I never commanded" (Jer. 7:30).

God concludes ever so softly that the wise, the strong, and the rich should not glory in wisdom, strength, or riches. For only in the intimacy that comes from knowing God may one boast (Jer. 9:23-24(22-23תנ"ך).

How ironic that God tells Yirm'yahu in advance that the people will neither listen nor repent of their sins (Jer. 7:21, 27). Yet when repentance is missing, the chatta't (*purification offering*) fails to purify even unintended sin. Devastating consequences follow! (See Jer. 7:28-8:3.)

? Have you ever attempted to placate God, but your heart was far from Him? To what degree can your efforts satisfy God or your conscience? What steps can you take to break out of dry times, when your heart is far from God?

Face to Face

" . . . so also the Messiah, having been offered once to bear the sins of many, will appear a second time, not to deal with sin, but to deliver those who are eagerly waiting for him. " —*Hebrews 9:28*

The blood of Messiah provides access to God, by purifying, consecrating, and sanctifying a New Covenant priesthood.

Under the "old" covenant, the sacrificial blood of animals consecrates by cleansing. Intentional sins are not decisively covered, however, and so conscience is not purged. The repetitive nature of the Yom Kippur ritual, to effect the removal of sins year after year, actually augments problems of conscience as the intentional sins of the nation pile up during the year. Furthermore, only the formally clothed and anointed representative of the nation has direct access to the living Presence of God.

Celebrate your freedom to enter God's Presence clothed in Messiah.

In contrast, Messiah's once-and-for-all sacrifice decisively purges conscience (Heb. 9:13-14). His death, ascension, and appearance "before the face of God" forever changes the nature of worship (Heb. 9:28). Now a royal priesthood has unlimited access to God.

? *Read Hebrews 9:28 again. Is the saving work of Messiah on behalf of a redeemed community or for individuals as New Covenant priests? Explain why He will appear again "without reference to our sins?"*

Talk Your Walk . . .

God tells Moshe: TSAV (*command!*) the priests to be made holy for priestly service. The very name "Leviticus" suggests that the book is a manual for instructing priests in performance of the priestly rituals. This portion describes priestly procedural commands for the olah (*ascent*), minchah (*tribute*), chatta't (*purification*), asham (*reparation*), and zevach sh'lamim (*sacrifice of well-being*). The order of the offerings moves from the most sanctified to offerings of lesser sanctity. The priests learn to attend to the most holy things first!

Priests are set apart and trained to perform priestly rituals.

The priestly rituals are designed to keep the Tent of Meeting pure and holy, set apart for the LORD. Each day, the Kohen Gadol offers a minchah as the tamid (*daily offering*). No other offerings are admissible until the Kohen Gadol, on behalf of the nation, draws near to offer a minchah (*tribute*) to God.

The kohanim (*priests*) are purified, anointed, ordained, and set apart. All commands are carried out with exacting attention to the most minute of details.

The portion ends with the Kohen Gadol waiting seven days to fulfill the time of ordination. He eats the ram and matzah as he waits, knowing that he is raised up (anointed with olive oil and sprinkled with blood) and made holy (set apart to God) to perform the most holy service of removing sins on behalf of the nation.

Oasis

. . . Walk Your Talk

The call to holiness is commanded for all who would minister for the nation as priests. Not just Aharon, but his sons also are sequestered during the time of ordination. Ask yourself honestly: when is the last time you set aside the week solely for the purposes of purifying yourself and seeking the face of the LORD?

Remember that you have unlimited access to God in heaven, right now! When Yeshua came, the entrance into God's dwelling in heaven was opened up for us. In the Spirit, we have been granted an access to God previously experienced by only the Kohen Gadol of the nation and by him only once each year. Do you take this privilege with anywhere near the holiness that God expressly commands?

Never forget that God is holy! And never forget that His Ruach haKodesh (*Holy Spirit*) dwells within your earthly tabernacle (1 Cor. 6:19-20). Give of your whole self in service. You will please Him with your offering—a sweet-smelling savor like the olah (*ascent offering*) and priestly minchah (*tribute*) that ascend to heaven itself.

New Covenant priests must give themselves wholly to serve God.

Shabbat Shalom!

שמיני tells us
that on the eighth day,
HaShem sent His fire
in a mighty way.
It fell on the altar,
making smoke from fillet.
We fell down and shouted,
"GOD IS THE WAY!"

Nadav and Avihu
took coals in a pan.
They offered to God
"strange fire" by hand.
God responded with fire,
Aaron's sons fell dead!
"I shall be glorified!"
was all HaShem said.

Walk Sh'mini!
9:1-11:47

Eighth

Torah—Leviticus 9:1-11:47

1st Call the Ordained—Leviticus 9:1
2nd Sacrifice Daily—Leviticus 9:17
3rd Consumed by Fire!—Leviticus 9:24
4th Eat the Minchah!—Leviticus 10:12
5th Render Holy Service—Leviticus 10:16
6th Avoid Impurity—Leviticus 11:1-2
7th Observe Ritual Purity—Leviticus 11:33
Maftir Make Distinctions—Leviticus 11:47

Haftarah—2 Samuel 6:1-7:17

David, not Sha'ul—2 Samuel 7:17

B'rit Chadashah—Hebrews 7:1-19

Melchi-Tsedek, not Aharon—Hebrews 7:18-19

Day Eight . . . After Ordination

Looking Back

In the book of Exodus, God makes a four-fold promise to bring us out of Egypt, to deliver us from bondage, to redeem us as a people, and to take us to be His people while we take Him to be our God. Four cups commemorate these promises at the Passover seder.

Moving to the book of Leviticus, **VAYIKRA** ADONAI (*and the LORD called*) us to bring sacrifices and draw near. He teaches us to bring the olah (*ascent offering*) exclusively for Him; the minchah (*grain offering* or *tribute*) for God and the priests; and the sh'lamim (*well-being* or *fellowship offering*) for God, the priests, and worshippers, too.

Then God tells Moshe, "**TSAV** (*command*) the kohanim (*priests*) . . . " They must follow legal, ritual procedures to receive our offerings and keep His dwelling pure and holy.

VAYIKRA—and the LORD calls us
to come into the Tent
and be holy for Him.

The LORD tells Moshe,
TSAV—command the priests
to be consecrated for ordination.
Seven days they spend
in God's Holy Presence.

Then ba-yom ha-SH'MINI,
on the eighth day,
the priests begin their work!
They keep the tabernacle
pure and holy,
the place where God dwells
among His people.

Certain portions of the offerings are specially designated for the kohanim. To ensure Yisra'el's offerings are acceptable to God, the kohanim celebrate life with God. They complete the atonement by eating, in a pure state and

Log

in a holy place, the offerings of the people. Then the priests lead by example, remaining "in communion" with the LORD.

Ba-yom ha-**SH'MINI** (*on the eighth day*), the time of ordination for the priests is completed. Now, those who are elevated to draw near to God on behalf of the nation initiate the first service of the tabernacle.

Scarcely is the service completed when the LORD sends a pillar of fire from heaven to consume offerings on one altar and incense on the other. The people shout and fall on their faces in glorious worship! It is apparent to all that God, as promised, has descended to dwell in the midst of His holy people, Yisra'el . . .

In SH'MINI . . .

The Key People are Moshe (*Moses*), Aharon (*Aaron*), Nadav (*Nadab*) and Avihu (*Abihu*), Misha'el (*Mishael*) and Eltsafan (*Elzaphan*), El'azar (*Eleazer*) and Itamar (*Ithamar*).

The Scene is the tabernacle, in the wilderness of Sinai.

Main Events include Aharon's first offerings; Moshe and Aharon entering the tabernacle; the glory of the Lord appearing; fire consuming the burnt offering; the people falling on their faces; Nadav and Avihu offering unauthorized fire and dying; El'azar and Itamar distinguishing holy from unholy and pure from impure.

The Trail Ahead

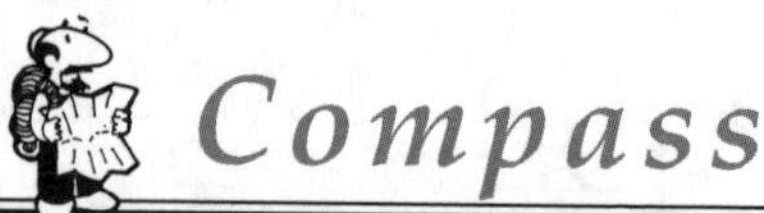

The Path

	י	נִ	י	מִ	שְׁ
letter:	yod	nun	yod	mem	shin
sound:	EE	**Nee**	EE	Mee	SH'

eighth = **SH'MINI** = **שמיני**

Work

The Legend

and it was	*va-y'hi*	וַיְהִי
on day the <u>eighth</u>	*ba-yom ha-<u>sh'mini</u>*	בַּיּוֹם הַשְּׁמִינִי
called Moses	*kara Moshe*	קָרָא מֹשֶׁה
to Aaron	*l'Aharon*	לְאַהֲרֹן
and to sons-his	*ool'vanav*	וּלְבָנָיו
and to elders of Israel	*ool'ziknei Yisra'el*	וּלְזִקְנֵי יִשְׂרָאֵל׃

—*Leviticus 9:1*

Related Words

eight	*sh'moneh*	שְׁמוֹנֶה
eighty	*sh'monim*	שְׁמוֹנִים
octave (also a stringed instrument, Ps. 6:1, 12:1)	*sh'minit*	שְׁמִינִית
18; 18 benedictions	*sh'moneh esreh*	שְׁמוֹנֶה עֶשְׂרֵה
8th day after Sukkot, a solemn assembly	*sh'mini atsehret*	שְׁמִינִי עֲצֶרֶת
8 garments (of the High Priest)	*sh'monah kelim*	שְׁמוֹנָה כֵּלִים
marriageable at 18	*sh'moneh esreh l'chupah*	שְׁמוֹנֶה עֶשְׂרֵה לְחֻפָּה

Hit the Trail!

Call the Ordained

"On the eighth day, Moshe called Aharon, his sons and the leaders of Isra'el . . ."

—Leviticus 9:1

Rosh Chodesh of Nisan, the first day of the civil year, Moshe calls the ordained. Aharon and his sons have completed the seven-day inaugural service. baYom haSH'MINI (*on the eighth day*), the priests enter the tabernacle to minister for the first time.

Day eight is the first day of a new week, a new year, and a new creation.

A time of transcendence begins! Tradition commemorates this day as the first day of creation. (Christians will later ascribe to resurrection Sunday the transcendent idea of the new creation.)

On this day, the kohanim perform the first sacrificial service of the nation. Heavenly fire consumes the altar offering. Individuals may no longer sacrifice meat on private altars. Now, priests eat of the meat of the chatta't (*purification offering*). Aharon concludes the first service with the Aaronic Benediction [Shabb. 87a]. Completion of the mishkan (*dwelling*) highlights the glorious appearing of the LORD among His people (Ex. 25:8, Lev. 9:4).

? ***Read Lev. 9:1, 4-6, 23. What is the purpose of this day? Review the role of the elders at Sinai (Ex. 24:5, 9-11). Explain why both elders and priests bring sh'lamim (fellowship offerings) to celebrate the LORD's appearing.***

Sacrifice Daily

“ The grain offering was presented; he took a handful of it and made it go up in smoke on the altar, in addition to the morning's burnt offering. ”

—Leviticus 9:17

Scooping three fingers of grain, Aharon the Kohen Gadol “fills his palm with it” and smokes it. Thus, the minchah accompanies the daily olah as the first offering of each morning (Ex. 29:40).

Sacrifice the daily offering to start and end each day.

Here, the Kohen Gadol offers the first “in-communion” gift. Previously, Aharon offered “out-of-communion” purification offerings for himself and for the people (Lev. 9:8-16). Rashi indicates that the egel (*calf, young bull*) atones for Aharon's role in the sin of the golden calf [Bav. Metzia 107b]. As at Sinai, the ascent and fellowship offerings are offered and eaten. But this time, Moshe enters the Tent with Aharon!

For the first time, someone other than Moshe approaches God in the Tent. Aharon, on behalf of all the people, draws near in sacred worship. Moshe and Aharon emerge together and bless the people. Immediately, God's Glory “is seen” by the entire people (Lev. 9:23).

? *Read Lev. 9:6, 17; Ex. 29:38-42; and Num. 28:2-8. Explain the purpose of the tamid or daily offering. Next, study Romans 12:1. How does the daily olah honor God? Explain why no other sacrifice can precede the daily olah.*

Consumed by Fire!

" Fire came forth from the presence of ADONAI, consuming the burnt offering and the fat on the altar. When all the people saw it, they shouted and fell on their faces. "
—Leviticus 9:24

Joyous blessing concludes the first sacrificial service. Aharon raises his hands to give the first Birchat Kohanim (*Aaronic Benediction*) [Lev. 9:22; Sot. 38a; Num. 6:24-26].

Aharon offers the olah, and God sends fire from heaven to consume it.

Fire falls from heaven, says the Sifra. The fire enters the Holy of Holies, consuming the incense offerings on the golden altar and roasting the olat tamid (*daily offering*) and the fat parts on the copper altar [Rashbam].

The spirit of holiness comes upon the people, and all sing out in praise of God! The people fall to their faces.

Another "eighth day" comes to mind. Sh'mini Atseret, the last holy convocation day of the Torah (Num. 29:35-40), when God dwells with His people and Torah is fulfilled. But this day awaits consummation; instead, Nadav and Avihu, in their excitement to draw near to God, offer esh zarah (*strange fire*). This breach of holiness costs them their lives (Lev. 10:1-2), as God's fire consumes them!

? *Study Lev. 10:10. The priest must distinguish kodesh (holy) from chol (common) and tahor (pure) from tamei (impure). Kodesh and tamei are contagious states which explode when mixed. Compare and contrast Lev. 9:24, 10:1-3.*

Eat the Minchah!

“Moshe said to Aharon and to El’azar and Itamar, his remaining sons, “Take the grain offering . . . and eat it without leaven next to the altar, because it is especially holy.” ***”*** ***—Leviticus 10:12***

Moshe reels from the catastrophic deaths of Aharon’s first-born and second-born. As the time for the first sacrificial service draws near, the nation is in utter disarray. The holy courts are tamei (*impure*) from corpse contamination! Moreover, the minchah (*tribute*) is uneaten (cf. Lev. 6:14-18(7-11תנ״ך)), and the priestly portion of the sh’lamim (*fellowship offering*) remains uneaten as well (Lev. 10:13-14).

Moshe directs the priests to eat the minchah to complete the dedication of the tabernacle. Eating the minchah and the breast/thigh portions from the sh’lamim honors the kohanim for their part in the ceremony. In Lev. 10:12, Moshe calls the uneaten minchah kodesh kodashim (*especially holy*).

Moshe orders the priests to complete the inauguration ceremony.

It is the priests’ job to present the minchah (*grain offering, tribute*) and to smoke the azkarah (*memorial portion*) on the altar as an offering to the Lord (Lev. 9:4, 17; 2:2-3).

? Aharon and his remaining sons mourn the loss of Nadav and Avihu. Read Lev. 10:6-7, 17. Since an onen (mourner) is forbidden to eat offerings, why does Moshe order the priests to eat the priestly portions? (Hint: note page 142.)

Render Holy Service

" Then Moshe carefully investigated what had happened to the goat of the sin offering and discovered that it had been burned up. He became angry with El'azar and Itamar . . . " —*Leviticus 10:16*

Purification requires offering three he-goats: two kodshei sha'ah (*one-time sacrifices,* lit. *holy things of the hour*) to inaugurate the sanctuary (Lev. 9:3); and a third, as chatta't (*purification*), recurring with each new moon [Lev. 10:17, Sifra, Shev. 9b, Num. 28:15].

Moshe fears that the priests are not rendering holy service to God.

Moshe is angry that the priests burned but did not eat the chatta't [Pes. 82b]. Inquiring insistently, he believes that the community's sins will not be expiated until the priests eat the third chatta't (Lev. 10:18).

Aharon responds that, in light of the deaths of his sons, he has exercised caution in performing priestly duties. As an onen (*mourner*), the priest cannot eat kodshei dorot (*permanent sacrifices,* lit. *holy things of the generations*), such as this third offering (Lev.R. 13:1). Aharon lacks the joy and tranquillity required to complete the atonement [Rashbam]. Satisfied, Moshe relents [Lev. 10:20; Rashi, Zev. 101a].

? *Two words, "darosh darash" (carefully investigated), mark Torah's exact midpoint (Lev. 10:16). The sages conclude that Torah requires searching inquiry. Was Moshe wrong to be angry? Defend your answer (cf. Mt. 5:23-24).*

Avoid Impurity

> *"ADONAI said to Moshe and Aharon, "Tell the people of Isra'el, 'These are the living creatures which you may eat among all the land animals . . ." "*
>
> *—Leviticus 11:1-2*

Torah classifies life into two broad categories—those who eat blood and those who don't. Land animals are further sub-divided into four areas: ruminants (non-blood-eaters or "cud-chewers") who fully split the hoof; ruminants who don't; non-ruminants who fully split the hoof; and the rest.

Ruminants that split the hoof are reiach nichoach (*a sweet savor*) to the LORD and also kosher (*fit*) for consumption by members of God's household, who should avoid becoming tamei (*impure*).

Thus, cattle, sheep, and goats are fit both for priestly food and for sacrifices. All other animals are not, including ruminant wannabes (camels, rabbits) and non-ruminant look-alikes (pigs).

Kosher practices elevate a kingdom of priests.

Following kosher laws maintains ritual purity in the camp. Individuals who contract ritual impurity must refrain from entering God's Presence until repurified through ritual procedures.

? ***Read Lev. 11:45. The LORD "brought us up" from Egypt—not "brought us out." Now read Lev. 11:3. Here, the cow "brings up" the cud! Explain why Torah uses terms from kashrut to explain our elevation as a people from Egypt.***

Observe Ritual Purity

❝ If one of them falls into a clay pot, whatever is in it will become unclean, and you are to break the pot. ❞

—Leviticus 11:33

Unclean objects, tools, and utensils can contaminate people, spreading pollution throughout the camp. Earlier, Torah dealt with how carcasses contaminate people by touch. Now, Torah gives rules on contamination of objects. Ritual purity laws regulate the process.

Cleanse or destroy all polluted objects.

Pots function by containing liquids. Holding unclean liquids or dead bugs pollutes the pot! Contamination comes from interior, not exterior, contact. Tum'ah (*contamination*) occurs even without contact, whether a corpse lying in a room or a fly caught in a jar.

The remedy for contamination of people calls for immersion in mikveh (*a body of living water*) [Rashi, commenting on the spring in Lev. 11:36]. In the case of a cheap clay pot, however, the porous nature absorbs uncleanness and makes cleansing it impossible. Therefore, the pot must be smashed or destroyed completely. In other words, porous pots that cannot be purified become vessels of destruction!

? *Read Romans 9:20-24. Rav Sha'ul describes men, headed for judgment, as vessels of destruction! Read Mk. 1:40-45; 7:18-23. In matters of ritual contamination, what did Messiah clarify?*

Make Distinctions

“ Its purpose is to distinguish between the unclean and the clean, and between the creatures that may be eaten and those that may not be eaten. ”

—Leviticus 11:47

Summary statements characterize maftir (*concluding*) readings. Here, the kohanim must distinguish tamei (*impure*) from tahor (*ritually pure*), and creatures that may and may not be eaten by a priestly people (Lev. 11:46-47).

The literary structure of chapter 11 parallels the tamei/tahor distinctions practiced in the camp, with the tahor in the center (Lev. 11:24-40) and the tamei around the periphery [Hartley, p. 155; note, Lev. 11:13-23, 41-45]. God resides in the ritually pure area at the camp's center.

Interestingly, the term "kosher" does not appear in the Torah. Yet priests minister by making these distinctions: between tam (*whole*) and tum'ah (*contaminated*), tahor (*pure*) and tamei (*impure*).

God elevates priests to distinguish between the holy and unholy.

In this way, Yisra'el as a nation adopts a lifestyle that sanctifies all creation. Practicing kashrut (*kosher laws*) and holiness elevates the nation [Sforno, Lev. 11:45]. Such priestly duties are also prophesied for the future (Ez. 44:23).

? Read Lev. 11:3, 45-46. Recall that Yisra'el has been "brought up" from the house of slavery. To fit into God's house, Yisra'el must be holy. Explain how Yisra'el sanctifies higher forms of life (animals, fowl, then swarmers).

David, not Sha'ul *Meander*

"Natan told David all of these words and described this entire vision."

—2 Samuel 7:17

Uzzah approaches too close to the holy ark and dies. David hastily orders the ark, meant to be carried on priestly shoulders, onto a wagon [Num. 4:15, 7:9; 2 Sam 6:3, 6-7; Antiq. 7.4.2].

The meek and humble, not the high and mighty, inherit the earth.

Yet God establishes the house of David forever! How ironic that Uzzah would be punished for David's failure to follow ritual procedure. Instead, the overlooked seventh son of Yishai (*Jesse*) displaces the house of Sha'ul (*Saul*), the Benjamite, with its hopes for a lasting dynasty.

Moreover, through Natan (*Nathan*) the prophet, God tells David that, though *he* cannot build an indestructible house for God (1 Chron. 17:4-5), God will build *him* an indestructible "house" (1 Chron. 17:11, 14-17).

Alas, David's son will build the house. A line of kings will issue from David's loins. Indeed, the house, kingdom, and throne shall be established eternally (2 Sam. 7:16), though not without interruption (Jer. 29:16-23, 30:8-9; Lk. 1:31-33).

? ***Read Romans 11:1. Notice that Sha'ul of Tarsus (Paul, the apostle to the nations) is a Benjamite. Explain the irony that God chooses an outcast king's son to take the Good News to the nations concerning Yeshua.***

...*ings* Melchi-Tsedek, not Aharon

"Thus, on the one hand, the earlier rule is set aside . . . and, on the other hand, a hope of something better is introduced, through which we are drawing near to God."* —*Hebrews 7:18-19

Aharon's line endures through two temples. Ultimately, a permanent priesthood, the spiritual priesthood of Melchi-Tsedek (*Melchizedek*), grants access to God's throne in heaven.

God establishes an eternal priesthood in Melchi-Tsedek.

An early Jewish hymn sings of the eternal heavenly origin of Melchi-Tsedek, a man whose beginnings are not in Torah, not in the world. Melchi-Tsedek has no predecessor in office. He is the first priest, and he is the one to whom Avram tithed with Levi still in his loins (Heb. 7:3-5, cf. Gen. 14:17-20).

Possibly the priesthood of Levi, with its laws of ritual purity, can achieve a formal wholeness to perfect the outer man (Heb. 7:11). But cleansing conscience and purity of the inner man requires even more (Heb. 9:6-10, 13-14; 10:1-18). The order of Melchi-Tsedek addresses these hopes. Access to God in heaven is not lost, because Messiah clothes us in righteousness. Put off deeds of the flesh! Put on the deeds of Messiah (2 Cor. 5:1-5).

***?** The principles for drawing near to God remain, but the substance by which we can realize our hopes changes. We need glorified bodies to live forever (1 Cor. 15:53-54). Does our weakness make Aharon's line a straw man? Explain.*

Talk Your Walk . . .

Ba-yom ha-**SH'MINI** (*on the eighth day*), Moshe calls Aharon, his sons, and the elders. After a seven-day inauguration, Aharon begins his first official service as Kohen Gadol (*High Priest*) of the nation. He sacrifices first for the priests, and then for the people whom he also blesses. Now fully consecrated, Aharon enters the tabernacle. When he comes out, he again blesses the people. The glory of the LORD consumes the offerings, and the people shout loudly and fall to the ground!

> ***As day eight begins, God's Presence rests upon His people.***

To complete the consecration, Moshe orders the priests to eat the sacrifices of the people. But two of Aharon's sons die, offering "strange" fire which does not issue from a divine origin. God demands exacting obedience, most particularly from those closest to Him. Failure to observe ritual purity laws kindles God's wrath, killing Nadav and Avihu!

The two remaining sons burn the purification offerings of the people, including the regular, daily offering. The kohanim must distinguish clean from unclean, and holy from unholy. God elevates His priests to serve in the sanctuary and to follow the laws of ritual purity so the LORD'S tabernacle remains holy. Moshe fears that, by not eating the sacrifices, the priests are disobeying God's command. But as onanim (*mourners*), Aharon's sons are not permitted to eat the monthly sacrifice.

Oasis

. . . Walk Your Talk

The worshipper approaches God to bestow glory on the only One who is worthy to receive it. The wise men came from afar to worship Yeshua (Mt. 2:2), who entered creation to "tabernacle" among men (Jn. 1:14). Circumcised and named "Yeshua" (*Salvation*) on the eighth day (Lk. 2:21), he later consecrated Himself for ministry, being set apart by Yochanan (Jn. 3:15-16).

In His last earthly prayer, Yeshua prayed for us to behold His glory (Jn. 17:24; Lev. 9:4, 6). Future prophecy reveals that God's glory alone will light the city of the LORD in New Jerusalem, which will descend from heaven to a completely new earth (Rev. 21:1-2, 23).

Are you consecrating yourself daily to enter God's Presence? At the final convocation, Sh'mini Atseret, God will tarry with those who are holy to Him. Is your spiritual self being transformed into the image and glory of God's everlasting Son (Ro. 8:29-30)? Your olah ascends daily. Each day, the standards of holiness in your life tighten, as you draw nearer to the time when God will manifest His glory. Is your inner man being sanctified to enter God's Presence?

Beyond death, you are called to live forever in the Presence of God.

Shabbat Shalom!

Now תזריע means
when a woman "bears seed,"
childbirth makes her unclean.
So take heed!
The sin offering purifies,
to clean all in need.
The olah goes straight up to God,
yes indeed!

A man may be smitten
with a skin affliction,
full of white hairs
and a raw spot that's itchin'.
The kohen looks closely,
and if it's no fiction,
the afflicted is banned.
It's a camp restriction!

Walk TAZRIA!
12:1-13:59

She bears seed

TORAH—Leviticus 12:1-13:59

1st Contain Impurity—Leviticus 12:1-2a
2nd Banish Tsara'at—Leviticus 13:6a
3rd Inflammations—Leviticus 13:18-19
4th Burns—Leviticus 13:24-25a
5th Scalls—Leviticus 13:29-30a
6th Baldness—Leviticus 13:40
7th Tsara'at on Garments—Leviticus 13:55
Maftir The Torah of Tsara'at—Leviticus 13:59

HAFTARAH—2 Kings 4:42-5:19a

Cleansing Tsara'at—2 Kings 5:19a

B'RIT CHADASHAH—Luke 7:18-35

Cleansing the Outcast—Luke 7:35

Seed-Bearing, Uncleanness, and Separation

Looking Back

VAYIKRA ADONAI (*and the LORD called*) us to be holy, approaching Him with gifts and offerings. He teaches us to bring the olah (*ascent offering*) exclusively for Him; the minchah (*tribute*) as a gift to God and the priests; and the sh'lamim (*well-being offering*) for God, the priests, and the worshippers, too.

God then tells Moshe, TSAV (*command!*) the priests to learn the rituals so they can keep the sanctuary holy.

Ba-yom ha-SH'MINI (*on the eighth day*), the service of the sanctuary will commence. Scarcely is the first service completed when the LORD sends a pillar of fire to kindle offerings on both altars. The people shout and fall on their faces in glorious worship! All know, on that day, that the LORD has appeared in the midst of His people.

VAYIKRA ADONAI from the Tent
and tells Moshe . . .
TSAV the priests
to learn the ritual procedures.

Then on SH'MINI, the eighth day,
the ordained may begin
to distinguish clean from unclean.

When a woman TAZRIA,
bears seed and births a child,
she carries impurities
that need cleansing . . .
or unholiness
will drive the LORD
from the midst of the camp!

But the camp must be kept pure for a holy God to dwell among His people. A woman who TAZRIA (*bears seed*) and gives birth to a son is tam'ah (*ritually impure*) for the week to come. On the eighth day, she can resume sexual relations with her husband; but

Log

In TAZRIA . . .

The Key People are Moshe (*Moses*), Aharon (*Aaron*), and Aharon's sons.

The Scene is the tabernacle, in the wilderness of Sinai.

Main Events include the LORD speaking to Moshe concerning women at childbirth; purification; various skin diseases; the role of the priest as hygiene inspector; unclean people dwelling outside the camp; and procedures to follow in examining fabric with mildew.

she must refrain from entering the sanctuary or consuming minchah offerings designated for priests and their families.

If she bears a daughter, her time of ritual impurity doubles. Some may cite this as an example of Torah's anti-feminine bias. Bonding with daughters who themselves nurture future infants, however, may reflect Torah's wisdom and God's love for the bearers of human life. Tradition ascribes the additional forty days to carrying the burden for a future mother.

When the time of ritual impurity ends, the mother presents an offering to complete the rites of purification. If she is a member of a priestly house, she can now resume eating the minchah.

Others with impurities are not so fortunate. Persons smitten by God (for offenses such as slander, gossip, arrogance, swearing false oaths, etc.) break out with tsara'at (*skin infection*). If purification procedures are ineffective, priests declare the smitten as tam'u (*ritually impure*) and ban them from the camp—perhaps for a lifetime . . .

The Trail Ahead 

The Path

	עַ	י	רִ	זְ	תַ
letter:	ayin	reish	reish	zayin	tav
sound:	(silent)-ah	EE	**Ree**	Z	Tah

she bears seed = TAZRIA = תזריע

The Legend

and spoke the LORD	*va-y'da**ber** ADONAI*	וַיְדַבֵּר יְהוָה
to Moses to say	*el-Mo**she** le**mor***	אֶל־מֹשֶׁה לֵּאמֹר׃
speak	*da**ber***	דַּבֵּר
to the sons of Israel	*el-b'**nei** Yisra'**el***	אֶל־בְּנֵי יִשְׂרָאֵל
to say	*le**mor***	לֵאמֹר
a woman who bears seed	*i**shah** ki taz**ria***	אִשָּׁה כִּי תַזְרִיעַ
and births a male	*v'yal**dah** za**char***	וְיָלְדָה זָכָר
is unclean	*v'tam'**ah***	וְטָמְאָה
seven days	*shiv'**at** ya**mim***	שִׁבְעַת יָמִים
like the days of her period	*ki**mei** ni**dat***	כִּימֵי נִדַּת
she will remain unclean	*do**tah** tit'**ma***	דְּוֺתָהּ תִּטְמָא׃

—*Leviticus 12:1-2*

Related Words

seed, offspring	***zeh**ra*	זֶרַע
Jew (seed of Jacob)	***zeh**ra **Ya**'akov*	זֶרַע יַעֲקֹב
of the royal family	***zeh**ra m'loo**cha***	זֶרַע מְלוּכָה
Jezreel (God sows)	*Yizr'**eil***	יִזְרְעֶאל
arm, forearm, strength, power, shankbone	*z'**roa***	זְרוֹעַ
starry sky (sky sown with stars)	*sha**ma**yim z'ru'**im** kocha**vim***	שָׁמַיִם זְרוּעִים כּוֹכָבִים

Hit the Trail!

Contain Impurity

" *ADONAI said to Moshe, "Tell the people of Isra'el: 'If a woman conceives and gives birth to a boy, she will be unclean for seven days with the same uncleanness as in niddah . . .'"* ***"*** *—Leviticus 12:1-2a*

When a woman TAZRIA (*bears seed*) during pregnancy, the issue of human-caused impurity must be addressed.

Women do not sin by giving birth to children (Gen. 1:28). Nor do their subsequent rites of purification require laying on of hands, confession, an asham, or a different offering for the birth of a boy or girl.

But the loss of blood diminishes a mother's wholeness, rendering her incomplete and thus tam'ah (cf. Lev. 12:4, 5, 7). Only the passage of time restores her wholeness.

Covenant people must remove ritual impurity. For the first week (two weeks, if a girl is born), the mother's impurity is contagious to others and niddah (*separated*) (Lev. 12:2).

We must approach God in a state of ritual purity.

Thereafter, Torah requires the completion of a 40 or 80 day waiting period from the time of birth, a transitory time when the mother must refrain from entering the sanctuary or consuming the kodashim (*sacred offerings*).

? *Read Lev. 8:33-35 (cf. Lev. 12:2, 5, 7). Explain why newly appointed kohanim offer sacrifices of expiation during their week of consecration. Explain why it takes twice as long to make a bearer of future mothers whole.*

Banish Tsara'at

" On the seventh day the cohen is to examine him again, and if the sore has faded and it hasn't spread on the skin, then the cohen is to declare him clean . . . "
—Leviticus 13:6a

Tsara'at (*skin infection,* sometimes translated *leprosy* from the Greek word lepra) describes something quite different from Hansen's Disease or contagious leprosy. In this verse, a two-week quarantine ends because the sore's color fades and affliction has not spread.

Priests safeguard the purity of the sanctuary and of the nation.

Tsara'at is the visible manifestation of a contagious impurity which God will not tolerate in His house! Rabbinic Judaism attributed such impurities as arising from slander, bloodshed, false oaths, and immorality [Arach. 15b]. Prosecuting slander in the courts can be extremely difficult (Num. 12:9-10; Dt. 24:8-9); but left unchecked, slander can destroy a community! Priests check the person, declaring him tahor (*pure*) or tamei (*defiled*) [M. Neg. 3:1].

The loss of vital fluids or breach of holy barriers renders a person tamei, whether as a result of bleeding, seeping or raw sores, pus, or scaling of skin. The defiled are declared stricken with tsara'at and barred from camp.

***?** Read Lev. 13:12-13. If skin infection "sprouts" and turns the entire body white (e.g. leukoderma), the priest declares the afflicted pure! Explain how, in this instance, "spreading" confirms loss of pigmentation and not tsara'at.*

Inflammations

" If a person has on his skin a boil that heals in such a way that in place of the boil there is a white swelling or a reddish-white bright spot, it is to be shown to the cohen. " —Leviticus 13:18-19

The third set of tests addresses inflammations such as boils, blisters, and pustules not caused by burns. Priests have already been instructed on how to judge lesions (Lev. 13:2-8) and raw skin (Lev. 13:9-17).

Skin infections do not ban the afflicted unless the priest says so.

In this verse, the boil disappears, tsara'at *(skin infection)* remains, and so the man must present himself to the priest. Recall that boils, the sixth plague, "broke out" on the Egyptians. Then God Himself hardened Pharaoh's heart for judgment (Ex. 9:8-12).

In this segment, the priest must distinguish between a spreading skin infection and the natural process of healing and scarring of an area. The priest orders a seven-day quarantine (Lev. 13:21) and watches for evidence of spreading. If the discoloration stands (but doesn't spread), the man is declared tahor (*ritually pure*). The priest's declaration is final—even if the priest has misdiagnosed the hand of God!

***?** When priests misdiagnose, then infected people (who ought to be declared tam'u) are free to enter the sanctuary to present or even eat offerings before the LORD. Explain why Torah grants priests the power to get it wrong.*

Burns

“ Or if someone has on his skin a burn caused by fire; and the inflamed flesh where it was burned has become a bright spot, reddish-white or white, then the cohen is to examine it . . . ”—Leviticus 13:24-25a

Burns and inflammations are handled in the same way. The priest waits for evidences of healing and then examines each spot separately, not in combination.

Separate treatment has implications. For example, if a burn appears beside an inflammation, but neither is the size of a g'ris (*large bean*), then the skin infection is too small to be judged as tsara'at (*skin infection*) [Rashi, Sifra]. Yet evaluated together, the two afflictions are sufficient to ban the infected from camp, possibly for a lifetime!

Inspection procedures are detailed and tedious (e.g. Is it psoriasis, eczema, or favus on the site of the burn or scar? Is there a white hair or a deep infection? Is it spreading?).

Priests make fine discriminations to judge skin infections.

Some burns are judged tamei (Lev. 13:24-25); others not initially decisive call for a quarantine of a week before being re-examined and judged tamei (Lev. 13:26-27); the rest are initially not decisive, but later judged tahor (Lev. 13:28).

? Talmud says that God intervened to keep the community holy and would smite someone for slander (e.g. Miryam, Num. 12:9-10). Yet Torah never names God as the active subject. Is God the active or passive agent? Explain.

Scalls

"If a man or woman has a sore on the head or a man in his beard, then the cohen is to examine the sore . . ."

—Leviticus 13:29-30a

Twenty-one different times we read, "The priest shall examine" (Lev. 13:3, 5, 6, 8, 10, 13, 15, 17, 20, 25, 27, 30, 32, 34, 36, 39, 43, 50, 51, 55, 56).

Priests examine whether the scall is tahor or tamei.

Sometimes the subject is a woman, sometimes a man, sometimes both. Sometimes the priest judges the person tahor (*undefiled*), sometimes tamei (*contagiously impure*). Sometimes the priest waits, quarantines a week and judges on day sh'mini (*eighth*); sometimes the quarantine is extended another week.

In this case, the priest examines a netek (*scall*), a bald mark where hair has fallen out. To evaluate the surrounding hair, the priest orders the person shaved (Lev. 13:33). Only the hair immediately surrounding the netek is left unshaved.

If after two quarantine periods the netek area has not spread, the man's clothes are washed, and he is declared tahor (Lev. 13:34, 37). Now he can freely enter to serve in the house of God!

? ***Read Gen. 41:14. Yosef was tested and proven. When he was shaved, given clean clothes, and released, he rose to great stature in the house of Pharaoh. God tests those he loves. Has God tested you? Describe the circumstances.***

Baldness

"If a man's hair has fallen from his scalp, he is bald; but he is clean."

—Leviticus 13:40

Six tests for tsara'at (scaly *skin disease*) require priestly evaluation: child birth (Lev. 12:2-5); skin infections (Lev. 13:2-3, 9-11); scars (Lev. 13:18-20); burns (Lev. 13:24-25); and infections of the scalp or beard (Lev. 13:29-30).

Tsara'at is God's way to call people, publicly, to repentance and modesty.

But tests for skin disease with baldness begin with conditions that are clearly tahor (*ritually pure*) (Lev. 13:40-41). Baldness is quite public and noticeable. In addition, a person afflicted with any of the four shades of white lesions suffers public humiliation; for many judge that God has withheld mercy from one who is so afflicted.

Prerequisites for declarations of purity end. Priests inform the public. Then the man is summarily removed to spend his days alone, outside the camp, with unkempt hair and torn clothing, crying out, "Tamei! Tamei! (*Defiled! Defiled!*)" (Lev. 13:44-46). Unless his condition changes, the person so afflicted remains barred from the camp, forever!

? Read Lev. 13:45-46. Once the man is declared tamei, the person with the polluted condition must be banished from the camp. It appears that God's holiness and God's compassion for the lowly are at odds. Explain the outcome.

Tsara'at on Garments

"The cohen is to examine it after the stain has been washed, and if he sees that the stain has not changed . . . it is rotten, no matter whether the spot is on the outside or on the inside." *—Lev. 13:55*

Man-made garments can also be stricken with tsara'at. To say clothing can get "skin infection" shows the difficulty of describing tsara'at. Rather, tsara'at attacks boundary lines between holy and not-so-holy!

Analogical (non-western) thinking undergirds the Hebrew worldview. Clothing, like skin, covers the body. By analogy, clothing is treated in the same way as skin in matters of ritual purity. References to digging out the karachat (*baldspot* or inside of the cloth) and the gabachat (*forehead* or outside of the cloth) apply to afflictions both in garments and skin.

Tsara'at afflicts skin and skin coverings.

The priest examines the garment for spreading and declares it tamei. Otherwise, he orders a washing and quarantine (Lev. 13:50, 53-55) before issuing a final judgment. Should the infected area disappear, but reappear at a later time, then the whole garment is declared tamei and burned (Lev. 13:57).

? *Explain why Torah commands that a garment be summarily burned if a fresh tsara'at breaks forth. Why not repeat the steps for inspection? Read Gen. 38:24. Explain Y'hudah's remark to burn his pregnant daughter-in-law.*

The Torah of Tsara'at

"This is the law concerning infections of tzara'at in a garment . . . or in the threads or the woven-in parts, or in any leather item—when to declare it clean and when to declare it unclean." —Lev. 13:59

Cleansing the garment is the subject of the maftir (Lev. 13:57-59). Procedures for purifying the M'TSORA (*infected one*) will be explained in the portion to come (Lev. 14-15).

Torah details procedures for treating clothing.

An afflicted garment should be washed. If the mark fades or disappears, the garment can be purified. It need not be burned. However, anything that "mars the surface . . . destroying its original wholeness" [Hartley, p. 193] is examined as a nega (*affliction*).

If the nega has faded, the garment can be salvaged by digging into (or cutting out) the nega and removing it completely. Then, the unaffected part of the garment can be washed again. If the garment remains as is, the priest declares it tahor.

Thus, the "torah" (*instruction*) of the tsara'at (*skin infection*) of garments concludes, with an emphasis on a process designed to protect integrity and wholeness. God wants the whole man and the man whole.

***?** Coverings protect the wholeness and integrity of life. Skin must contain blood and vital fluids necessary for life; clothing guards integrity. Explain how both skin and clothing function as boundaries of holiness.*

Cleansing Tsara'at *Meander*

> *"Elisha said to him, "Go in peace.""*
>
> *—2 Kings 5:19a*

Na'aman, a ranking Syrian general, is infected with tsara'at (2 Ki. 5:1). Tradition says he was a great warrior but also arrogant and proud [Num. R. 7:4-5], and so God smote him. As a result, Na'aman approaches Elisha in modesty, coming with a small retinue (2 Ki. 5:9 refers to susav—*his horse,* not *horses*).

Na'aman had captured an Israelite girl, who suggests he go to Yisra'el for healing (2 Ki. 5:3). The king of Yisra'el responds, tearing his clothes, "Am I God?"—for only God can heal tsara'at (2 Ki. 5:7).

The haftarah cuts off in mid-verse (19a), before Na'aman starts "home." Perhaps Na'aman has a new home, given his new belief: ". . . there is no God in all the earth except in Isra'el!" (2 Ki. 5:15b).

Na'aman, cleansed of tsara'at, believes in Yisra'el's God.

Na'aman departs from Elisha in peace, taking two mule loads of the land of Yisra'el so that he can build an altar and offer sacrifices to the God of Yisra'el alone (2 Ki. 5:17, 19).

? *Explain how God's affliction draws Na'aman to see God's greatness. How does God break Na'aman's arrogance? Study 2 Ki. 5:18. Is Na'aman still an idolater?*

...ings Cleansing the Outcast

" Well, the proof of wisdom is in all the kinds of people it produces. "

—Luke 7:35

Yeshua quotes Isaiah 61:1 to Yochanan's disciples—the blind see, those with tsara'at are cleansed, the dead are raised, and the poor rejoice in the Good News (Lk. 7:22). If Yochanan can't see Yeshua as Messiah, then he is lacking wisdom! But wisdom knows her children (Lk. 7:35).

The rabbis have taught, "Four people are considered as if they are dead: a pauper, a leper, a blind man, and one who is childless" [Ned. 64b]. In fact, Talmud says that curing someone of tsara'at is the equivalent of raising him from the dead [Num. 12:12 in Sanh. 47a].

Messiah does this and more! He cleanses those who are most excluded from the activities of life and from the camp of Yisra'el, and he draws them near to God.

The socially ostracized glory in the newness of life that Messiah brings.

Yeshua's deeds offer hope to the social outcasts among the people (Is. 35:5-6). The walking dead jump for life!

? *Read Mark 1:40-45. Notice that Yeshua touches an unclean man and then tells him to follow the purifying procedures for m'tsora (Lev. 14). Explain who "sits alone" (Lev. 13:46). Comment on this paradox (Is. 53:4-6).*

Talk Your Walk . . .

A woman TAZRIA (*bears seed*) and gives birth, beginning the process of life anew! The baby enters creation clean; but the woman, losing wholeness, incurs impurity. She waits a week (or two), to resume sexual relations with her husband. After forty (or eighty) days, she offers a chatta't (*purification offering*) and an olah (*ascent offering*) to decontaminate herself so she can re-enter society.

Thus begins the portion that addresses impurities caused by man. Torah teaches the priests to distinguish tsara'at (*contagious skin infection*) from inflammations, burns, scalls (ripped hair), baldness, and marks on garments. Functioning as health inspectors, priests examine carefully and then declare persons and articles of clothing either tahor (*not contagious*) or tamei (*contagious*). If a judgment is not yet clear, then priests order a quarantine or undergo ritual procedures (shaving, cutting out, washing, etc.). They check again at a prescribed time (either immediately, or one to two weeks later) to make a final determination.

Priests must examine impurities to keep the nation holy before God.

In life, contagious impurity can afflict anyone, not just those who sin. Only the ritually pure have the freedom to enter the sanctuary where God dwells. To be "on call" to God requires a person to observe regulations of ritual purity at all times. If priests do their job, the nation maintains its state of ritual purity.

Oasis

. . . Walk Your Talk

Do you wish God's abiding Presence were more tangible to you? When God dwelt among His people in a physical way, ritual procedures had great importance. Persons could not knowingly enter the sanctuary in an impure condition. Such a sin would be tantamount to idolatry!

At Sinai, God elevated us as a priestly nation. For three days, all Yisra'el abstained from sexual relations to maintain ritual purity and prepare to meet with God. On day forty we broke the covenant, and it required an additional forty-day wait for a new set of tablets. This timing is analogous to a mother's forty (or eighty) day wait after birth. The rite of purification restores her wholeness and her access to God's house and covenant fellowship.

Do you have patience to wait upon God and fill up with His holiness? Time is a key ingredient for filling! Are you willing to set aside your sexual drives for a season and sublimate these energies to seek God's face? Chastity reflects a willingness to be "on call" to God at all times (1 Cor. 7:5-6). Are you willing to fast and pray for purposes of spiritual warfare? Do you wholeheartedly belong to God?

It takes time to devote oneself wholly to God.

Shabbat Shalom!

מצרע just means
"the one who's infected."
His impurity
must be dis-infected.
So the kohen offers a lamb
to deflect it,
and the unclean hopes
he'll be resurrected!

And if a house
gets infected walls,
the stones are scraped
so the spreading stalls.
If it breaks out again
inside the halls,
then stone by stone
the whole structure falls!

Walk M'TSORA!
14:1-15:33

Infected one

TORAH—Leviticus 14:1-15:33

1st The Day of Cleansing—Leviticus 14:1-2
2nd The Rite of Purification—Leviticus 14:13
3rd Cleansing the Poor—Leviticus 14:21
4th Cleansing Houses—Leviticus 14:33-35
5th Summary of Cleansing—Leviticus 14:54-57
6th Unclean Male Discharges—Leviticus 15:16
7th Unclean Female Discharges—Leviticus 15:29
Maftir Safeguarding God's House—Leviticus 15:31-33

HAFTARAH—2 Kings 7:3-20

The Camp Destroyed—2 Kings 7:20

B'RIT CHADASHAH—Matthew 23:16-24:2, 30-31

The Temple Destroyed—Matthew 24:31

Infection, Purification, and Re-Entry

Looking Back

Climbing Ya'akov's ladder to be with God in heaven is a calling of the nation of Yisra'el. But the nation's ascent is spiritual, through the priesthood.

VAYIKRA ADONAI (*and the LORD called*) Moshe to enter the Tent, where God has come down to dwell in our midst. He tells Moshe: TSAV (*command!*) the kohanim to receive offerings. They must keep the sanctuary holy by observing the rituals designed for cleansing.

Into the tabernacle go Aharon and his sons for a seven-day ordination. Then ba-yom ha-SH'MINI (*on the eighth day*), the priests begin the service of the sanctuary. Detailed instructions guide them, as they face the impurities of life itself while striving to maintain purity and dwell in the Presence of a holy God.

When a woman TAZRIA (*bears seed*) to bring about new life, she must undergo a cleansing process. These steps remove the uncleanness of the afterbirth and prepare her to re-enter the community.

VAYIKRA ADONAI from the Tent
and tells Moshe,
TSAV the priests to learn
the ritual procedures.
By day SH'MINI,
the ordained priests begin
their work, distinguishing
clean from unclean.

When a woman TAZRIA, she bears
impurities during childbirth—
not sinful, but in need of cleansing.
Afflicted by God,
the M'TSORA, infected one,
must receive healing
and ritual purification . . .
or remain excluded from the camp.

The M'TSORA (*infected one*) has been declared tamei (*ritually impure*). He must remain outside the camp until God heals him. The priest exits the camp to examine the m'tsora and carry out rites of purification, so the healed m'tsora may re-enter the community. The ritual describes rites of purification observed the first week (Lev. 14:2-9); rites for a second week if necessary (Lev. 14:10-20); and an alternative economic procedure for the poor (Lev. 14:21-34).

Contagious impurity can exclude all persons from their respective camps. Thus, pollution from physical contact with the dead excludes a High Priest from the Holy of Holies. Pollution from sexual relations with a niddah (*menstruant*) or zavah (*one discharging on non-menstrual days*) excludes a Levite from serving in the sanctuary. Finally, pollution from tsara'at (*contagious skin infection*) on clothing or flesh excludes an Israelite from living in the camp. But in most instances, with healing, the passage of time, and the observance of ritual purity procedures commanded by God, restoration is possible . . .

In M'Tsora . . .

The Key People are Moshe (*Moses*) and Aharon (*Aaron*).

The Scene is the tabernacle, in the wilderness of Sinai.

Main Events include procedures for dealing with skin diseases, rites of purification, and infection in stone houses; laws for people entering such places; and more laws about discharges, bathing, and the length of time of impurity. All regulations are designed to separate the children of Yisra'el from their uncleanness, so they do not walk in impurity or defile the altar of God's tabernacle.

The Trail Ahead

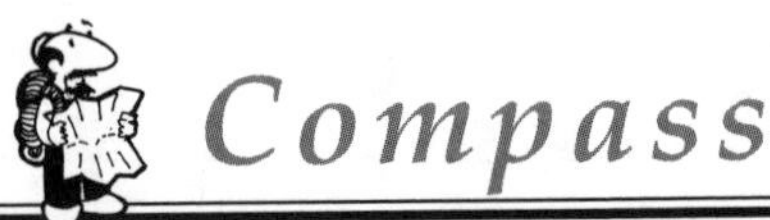

The Path

	ע	רָ	צֹ	מְ
letter:	ayin	reish	tsadee	mem
sound:	(silent)	**Rah**	TSoh	M'

infected one = **M'TSORA** = **מצרע**

The Legend

and spoke the LORD	*va-y'da**ber** ADONAI*	וַיְדַבֵּר יְהוָֹה
to Moses	*el-Mo**she***	אֶל־מֹשֶׁה
saying	*le**mor***	לֵּאמֹר׃
this will be	*zot tih'**yeh***	זֹאת תִּהְיֶה
instruction/law of	*to**rat***	תּוֹרַת
the <u>infected one</u>	*ha-<u>m'tso**ra**</u>*	הַמְּצֹרָע
on day (of)	*b'**yom***	בְּיוֹם
cleansing-his	*tahora**to***	טָהֳרָתוֹ
and he will be brought	*v'hoo**va***	וְהוּבָא
to the priest	*el-ha-ko**hen***	אֶל־הַכֹּהֵן׃

—*Leviticus 14:1-2*

Related Words

leper, leprous	*m'tso**ra***	מְצֹרָע
lepers' house	*beit m'tso**ra**'im*	בֵּית מְצֹרָעִים
leper hospital, leprosarium	*mitsra'**ah***	מִצְרָעָה
leprosy, (fig. plague, pest)	*tsa**ra**'at*	צָרַעַת
wasp, hornet	*tsir'**ah***	צִרְעָה

Hit the Trail!

The Day of Cleansing

" *ADONAI said to Moshe, "This is to be the law concerning the person afflicted with tzara'at on the day of his purification. He is to be brought to the cohen."* ***"***
—Leviticus 14:1-2

A person afflicted with a skin infection is described as M'TSORA (*the infected one*). Remember, the kohen (*priest*) does not heal; rather, he functions as a health inspector to determine whether the person is fit to live in the camp. If not, the priest declares the person tamei (*impure*) to enter the sanctuary, and in more serious cases, tamei to live in community.

The affliction must go away before a priest goes out to inspect (Lev. 14:3). To re-enter the camp, the m'tsora presents two live birds. One is slaughtered, and its blood is sprinkled seven times on the m'tsora. The other bird is set free. For seven more days, the m'tsora still transmits contagious impurity by contact. On day seven, the m'tsora launders, shaves, and bathes.

The kohen administers rites to purify a m'tsora to re-enter community.

The eighth day, the m'tsora brings an asham (*reparation*) with some oil, as a t'nufah (*elevation offering*) to God. Thereafter, applying the blood of the lamb and the oil sanctifies and restores the person to live in covenant community.

? ***Read Lev. 14:12, 18, Is. 53:10-12, and Mt. 26:6-13. Note the use of anointing oil in the house of Shim'on, healed of tsara'at. Explain why Yeshua says the oil prepared his body for burial. Explain how Yeshua, the lamb, is an asham.***

The Rite of Purification

> ❝ *He is to slaughter the male lamb at the place in the sanctuary for slaughtering . . . because the guilt offering belongs to the cohen, just like the sin offering; it is especially holy.* ❞ —*Leviticus 14:13*

Rites of purification cleanse and elevate the m'tsora to re-enter the avodah (*service, worship*) of the nation. The ritual procedure is analogous to the rites of ordination for consecrating priests and altars.

Blood from an unblemished, year-old, ewe lamb, slaughtered as an asham (*reparation*), is applied to the right ear, right thumb, and right big toe of the m'tsora (cf. Lev. 8:14-15, 22-25). Anointing the outer extremities—whether the horns of the altar; the ears, thumbs, and toes of a man; or for that matter, the holiest kohen and the most afflicted m'tsora—consecrates the whole to God!

Purifying the extremities purifies the whole.

The priest anoints the m'tsora with oil (Lev. 14:18, cf. Lev. 8:12). Offerings complete the rite—the chatta't purifies, the olah rededicates, and the minchah feeds the priests. Then the m'tsora can freely enter the camp to eat sh'lamim as a member of the community. Thus, the kohen declares the m'tsora tahor (*pure*) (Lev. 14:19-20).

? *Use Mt. 26:6-7, 12, Jn. 1:29, and Is. 53:7, 12 to explain how Yeshua could become a sin-bearer. Then read Lev. 19:17 and explain how Yeshua's silence (like a lamb) could also be God's way of making him bear our sins! How are we purified?*

Cleansing the Poor

"If he is poor . . . he is to take one male lamb as a guilt offering to be waved, to make atonement for him; two quarts of fine flour mixed with olive oil for a grain offering . . ." —*Leviticus 14:21*

The poor substitute birds for the lambs normally required as the chatta't (*purification offering*) and the olah (*ascent offering*). The asham (*reparation offering*), however, remains a year-old, unblemished, male lamb, costing rich and poor alike a large donation to make atonement.

The asham is the only offering that cannot be reduced in price.

Each lamb requires an accompanying minchah (*tribute*) of fine flour, about one day's ration. The minchah is important, because the newly restored m'tsora eats this grain offering in the presence of God, showing that his repentance is fully accepted by God.

To summarize, the purification offering and the olah can be reduced. Younger less expensive doves, or older and larger turtledoves can be substituted for those lambs on a "whatever is affordable" basis (Lev. 14:22). However, the asham and minchah are binding on rich and poor alike. There can be no substitute for the unblemished lamb in Torah's demand for an asham. Reparation must be paid in full!

? *Why do you suppose the asham is singled out as the only offering that must be a lamb? How can grace allow for cutting the price to the poor for the purification and the dedication offerings, but not for the reparation offering?*

Cleansing Houses

> ❝ *ADONAI said to Moshe and Aharon, "When you have entered the land . . . and I put an infection of tzara'at in a house . . . then the owner of the house is to come and tell the cohen . . . "* ❞ *—Lev. 14:33-35*

Tsara'at also infects houses! If these outbreaks recur, the house must be destroyed, stone by stone! Citing Sifra, Rashi comments that sometimes God would infect the walls of a captured Canaanite house to reveal hidden treasure within!

Even corporate coverings, such as houses, can get skin infection.

Before calling the kohen, the owner empties his house —so his belongings can escape being declared tam'u along with the structure (Lev. 14:36). The priest then quarantines the house for seven days.

The procedure for dealing with nega tsara'at (*affliction of skin infection*) of a house parallels the first stage in the purity ritual for persons (Lev. 14:4-9, 49-53). In both cases, a bird is slaughtered. Hyssop, cedar wood, and scarlet cloth are dipped in its blood, which is sprinkled seven times on the afflicted house or person and then on the second bird. This bird is set free to fly over an open field to complete the atonement (Lev. 14:53). The priest now declares the house tahor!

? *If the mildew reappears a second time, the house must be destroyed, stone by stone! (Lev. 14:44-45). Read Mt. 23:19, 25-38; 24:2. How could Yeshua declare that the second Temple must be demolished "with no stones left?"*

Summary of Cleansing

> *"Such is the law for all kinds of tzara'at sores, for a crusted area, for tzara'at in a garment, for a house . . . to determine when it is clean and when it is unclean . . . "* —*Leviticus 14:54-57*

The verses above conclude the long list of regulations spanning both the portions TAZRIA (*she bears seed*) and M'TSORA (*infected one*). It becomes clear that tsara'at (*infection*) is a God-given plague that can erupt on skin, clothing, or a house.

Tsara'at must be purified, or it infects the stones of the sanctuary.

The smitten person goes to the kohen, who examines the nega (*affliction*). Based on torah (*instruction*) for scabs, swellings, and shiny spots, the kohen declares the affliction tahor (*pure*) or tamei (*impure*). Thereafter, should God heal the nega, the kohen performs rites of purification to readmit the person to the sanctuary and the community.

According to the tradition, tsara'at stopped appearing after the destruction of the first Temple. When God's sanctuary was rebuilt, His Presence did not manifest in the same way—even though the Temple cost far more. Worship of false gods ended, but sinat chinam (*hatred for one's fellow man*) continued to grow. A spiritual solution was needed.

? ***Read Is. 53:7, 10. Scripture says that the Messiah offered himself as an asham and that God was pleased to afflict him. In what way have you been cleansed by Messiah's rite of purification in the heavenly places? (Heb. 10:10, 19-22).***

Unclean Male Discharges

❝ If a man has a seminal emission, he is to bathe his entire body in water; he will be unclean until evening. ❞

—Leviticus 15:16

Sexual purity is critical for approaching the sanctuary. In stark contrast to the fertility cults, God set high moral standards for His people.

The ba'al keri (*male with seminal emission*) is tamei (*impure*) until evening. He is not tahor (*pure*) to enter the sanctuary or eat holy offerings until after he has scrubbed, changed clothes, and awaited three stars to appear.

In the case of a second discharge in the same day, the ba'al keri is labeled zav (*one suffering from a discharge*). His clothing, bedding, and sitting furniture are contagious to others. After a seven day wait, the zav is tahor, but only after scrubbing and immersion [Zav. 1:1-4].

Unclean discharges bar a zav from entering the sanctuary for a week.

In the event of a third discharge within three successive days, the ba'al keri is a zav sheni (*zav, second time*). He must follow the same procedures as a zav; but on the eighth day, he must present a chatta't (*purification*) and an olah (*ascent*) to show gratitude for being cleansed.

***?** Seminal fluids are created with the potential to co-create life with the Creator. When not properly contained within holy boundaries, a tamei condition arises. Why would a holy God distance Himself and His house from a zav?*

Unclean Female Discharges

"On the eighth day, she is to take for herself two doves or two young pigeons and bring them to the cohen at the entrance to the tent of meeting."
—Leviticus 15:29

The terms "niddah" (*menstruant*) and "zavah" (*one-with-a-flow*) [Fox, p. 582] describe women in unclean states. Both must bathe, scrub clothes, and wait seven days to restore purity [Nidd. 41, 43, 51, 56].

Unclean discharges bar a zavah from the sanctuary for a week.

The zavah (*one who discharges on days other than menstruation*) can be k'tanah (*minor*) or g'dolah (*major*). In the analog of a zav sheni, the zavah g'dolah (*three flows in three successive days*) requires offerings on the eighth day for purification and rededication (two turtledoves or pigeons).

The chatta't (*purification*) atones for the zavah g'dolah. Kapparah (*atonement, covering*) prepares one's inner life to ascend from tahorah (*a state of purity*) to k'dushah (*a state of holiness*). Sacrifice ministers at a deeper level to address unconscious patterns of pollution [Munk, p. 169]. Cleansing impurities allows for access to the sanctuary, but growth in holiness keeps pollution from arising!

? *Immersion (mikveh) and then waiting until evening cleanses most normal conditions. Irregular conditions require rites of purification. Discuss similarities and differences between cleansing a zav sheni and a zavah g'dolah.*

Safeguarding God's House

" . . . separate the people of Isra'el from their uncleanness, so that they will not die . . . for defiling my tabernacle . . . Such is the law . . . for the person, man or woman, with a discharge . . . "—Lev. 15:31-33

Three zones of holiness separate the LORD from the nations: the most holy machaneh sh'chinah (*camp of the Glory*), the holy camp of the Levites, and the camp of Yisra'el.

Holiness limits *everyone's* access to God's Presence. The laity have no access to areas reserved for male kohanim, elevated by ritual to holy status. The camp of Levites, reserved for priests and their households, excludes the zav, zavah, niddah, and all that are not tahor. Finally, the boundaries of the camp separates Yisra'el from the nations, from the dead, and from those afflicted with tsara'at (*skin infection*). ADONAI, the Holy One of Yisra'el, dwells in His camp, meeting kohanim at the altar of incense and Yisra'el at the altar of olah (Ex. 29:43-46).

Impurity not rectified threatens the nation.

The priests keep the camp fit by distinguishing tahor (*pure*) from tamei (*impure*) and kadosh (*holy*) from chol (*common*). Kohanim perform rites of purification, lest contagious impurity defile the sanctuary, drive God from the camp, and lead to the death of the nation!

? Suppose someone buries a corpse, re-enters the camp in a tamei state, and touches a kohen. Unaware, the kohen goes on duty and eats a sacrifice. Contagious impurity defiles the sanctuary! What is the remedy for this occurrence?

The Camp Destroyed *Meander*

> ***"That is exactly what happened to him, because the people trampled him down in the gateway, so that he died."***
>
> *—2 Kings 7:20*

War between Aram (Syria) and Yisra'el threatens to destroy Yisra'el. Four outcast lepers lead a life of quiet despair, and yet they become saviors of their nation!

> ***In the day of salvation, those who are excluded shall be included.***

Afflicted with actual leprosy, these m'tsoraim (*infected ones*) suffer from a disease that eats away at the deeper layers of the skin. In Yeshua's time, leprosy killed its victims. Josephus describes m'tsoraim as "in effect dead persons" [Ant. 3:261].

Figuring they will die from the war-imposed famine, these four lepers go to the Aramean camp to beg food. They discover the place abandoned, with great supplies of food and wealth left behind. They begin to loot, but then they repent their actions and report the good news to Yisra'el. In the ensuing rush for food, the king's cynical advisor gets trampled at the gate—just as Elisha had foretold!

***?** Idolatrous ways eventually led to Yisra'el's destruction. Here, the individuals, afflicted by God, become heroes of the nation. Is there a connection between their repentance and exaltation? Explain.*

The Temple Destroyed

❝ He will send out his angels with a great shofar; and they will gather together his chosen people from the four winds, from one end of heaven to the other. ❞
—Matthew 24:31

Yeshua asks which is more important, the sacrifice or the altar. He clarifies that the altar makes the sacrifice holy, and not the reverse (Mt. 23:19)!

The sanctuary is defiled again, and every stone must be dismantled.

But Yisra'el has slain the prophets sent to call her back to the covenant—including Z'charyah (*Zechariah/"God remembers"*), the last mentioned in the Tanakh (2 Chr. 24:20). Worst of all, his blood splatters, defiling the ground between the altar and the Temple (Mt. 23:35; 2 Chr. 24:21-22; cf. Gen. 4:10). How, then, can the priest approach God from the altar?

Yeshua knew Z'charyah's dying words. He held the religious leaders of the Temple accountable for the redemption of all mankind—starting with Hevel (*Abel*), the first martyr, and ending with Z'charyah, the last in Tanakh (Mt. 23:36).

Y'rushalayim that stones the prophets will be left desolate! (Mt. 23:37-38). Every last stone of the rebuilt Temple must be thrown down!

***?** The nation of Yisra'el is judged unclean. Y'hudah is scattered among the nations—outside the camp. Read Is. 53:6-8, 10-11. Why does God smite the King of kings as His asham? making reparations for whom? for Hevel?*

Talk Your Walk . . .

The portion M'TSORA describes the rites of purification which the priests must perform upon those declared tamei (*ritually impure*) and then cleansed by God. The m'tsora (*infected one*) must bring a lamb for an asham (*reparation*), so that God will forgive his trespass for walking in impurity. God demands that His firstborn nation, a kingdom of priests, acknowledge and repent their unholy ways.

The rites of purification resemble the rites of ordination for the nation's priests. Blood and oil anoint the right ear, right thumb, and right toe in a manner analogous to the anointing of Aharon and his sons for priestly duty. After mandatory offerings, the purified worshipper is elevated and restored to life in the community.

Infection must be limited by following prescribed rites of purification.

Infections can also plague outward coverings, such as clothing and houses. If tsara'at (*infection*) reappears upon a house after it has been scraped, the entire house is leveled, stone by stone. Then the whole structure is removed and deposited outside the boundaries of the camp. One might wonder if the Temple suffered this fate, the day the Roman armies came and tore it down—stone by stone.

Oasis

. . . Walk Your Talk

Egyptian folklore surrounding the Exodus claims that the expulsion of Yisra'el can be traced to a people stricken with tsara'at [Ginzberg, p. 296, n.101]. Thirteen sins are punished by tsara'at. These include blasphemy, unchastity, murder, false suspicion, pride, unlawful acquisition of the rights of others, slander, theft, perjury, demeaning God's holy name, idolatry, envy, and contempt for Torah [Num. R. 7:4-5]. The midrash suggests that the "mark of Cain" is tsara'at [Num. R. 22:12-13]. Did Yisra'el sow and reap the sins of the nations the day it joined them at Calvary to murder the King of kings?

God accepted Yeshua's offer of His soul as an asham (Is. 53:10). Heirs abound! Both Jews and gentiles gain access to heaven when robed in the deeds of Messiah. As our reparation, Yeshua's sacrifice cleanses our inner man where conscience lives (Heb. 10:19). In what way does this enormous truth humble you, now that you draw near to serve the God of heaven and earth?

As high priests of earth, we intercede for the redemption of men.

"After the death" translates
"אחרי מות."
Atone for the altar
in a white linen coat.
On Yom Kippur,
cut a bull by its throat.
Go into God's Presence
with an unblemished goat!

Remember the truth
that the life's in the blood.
We all need atonement
to get rid of the crud!
For God is holy,
and our sins are like mud.
We must be washed clean,
or we'll die with a thud!

Walk Acharei Mot!
16:1-18:30

אחרי מות

After the death

Torah—Leviticus 16:1-18:30

1st Be Holy or Die!—Leviticus 16:1
2nd Cleanse the Sanctuary—Leviticus 16:18
3rd Purge Impurities—Leviticus 16:25
4th Consecrate Blood—Leviticus 17:1-2
5th Sanctify Life—Leviticus 17:8-9
6th Sanctify Family—Leviticus 18:6
7th Safeguard the House—Leviticus 18:22
Maftir Safeguard the Camp—Leviticus 18:30

Haftarah—Amos 9:7-15; Ezekiel 22:1-16

Sanctify the City—Ezekiel 22:15-16

B'rit Chadashah—1 Corinthians 6:9-20

Sanctify the Kingdom—1 Corinthians 6:20

After the Death,
Approach God in Holiness

Looking Back

VAYIKRA ADONAI (*and the LORD called*) Moshe to the Tent, explaining how Yisra'el may enter His Presence with offerings.

VAYIKRA ADONAI from the Tent and tells Moshe, TSAV the priests to learn ritual procedures . . . Then on day SH'MINI, they can distinguish clean from unclean.

When a woman TAZRIA, her impurities must be cleansed. The M'TSORA needs his infection healed and ritually cleansed . . . or else he will remain excluded from the camp.

ACHAREI MOT—after the death of Nadav and Avihu, the remaining priests approach God only according to strict ritual procedure.

He tells Moshe, TSAV (*command!*) the priests to follow orderly ritual procedures when receiving the offerings. Moshe consecrates the priests for seven days, to elevate them for holy service.

Ba-yom ha-SH'MINI (*on the eighth day*), the kohanim commence service in the sanctuary. But things go wrong! Aharon's sons, zealous to offer incense, jump ahead of orders; they die in the holy place.

Scripture devotes the next two portions to distinguishing tahor (*pure/not impure*) from tamei (*impure/contagious*). When a woman TAZRIA (*bears seed*), she remains ritually impure for a week. On the eighth day, she can resume sexual relations with her mate in the home; but she is still tam'ah to enter God's house or consume offerings designated for the priestly families. She must wait a total of 40 days (or 80 days from the birth of a daughter), before completing her days of

Log

filling, when she can approach the altar in a pure state.

In contrast, the M'TSORA (*infected one*) must be healed by God before he can be ritually cleansed. Otherwise, the infected one is barred indefinitely from the camp, crying, "Tamei! Tamei!"

ACHAREI MOT (*after the death*) of Nadav and Avihu, God restricts access to His holy Presence. He orders a yearly cleansing of the camp to restore purity and remove impurities introduced by sin. Respect for the sanctity of life requires all blood to be consecrated. Blood is holy, specially reserved for creating life, restoring purity, or removing impurity from the holy camp where the Holy One of Yisra'el dwells . . .

In ACHAREI MOT . . .

The Key People are Moshe (*Moses*), Aharon (*Aaron*) and sons, and the assembly.

The Scene is the tabernacle, in the wilderness of Sinai.

Main Events include advice to approach God carefully after the death of Aharon's sons; to follow the order of ritual specified in detail; to atone for the sanctuary (Tent of Meeting) and for the assembly (the people and the priests); information about Yom Kippur offerings; a reminder that the life is in the blood and there is only one place, the altar, for making sacrifices; the spiritual connection between the altar, the priests, and the assembly; advice to keep holy after all is cleansed and to avoid immoral behavior; warning that the land vomits out its unclean inhabitants; and the necessity of holiness so that God will continue to dwell in His nation.

The Trail Ahead 

The Path

וידבר יהוה אל משה
אחרי מות שני בני אהרן
בקרבתם לפני יהוה וימתו

—ויקרא יו/א

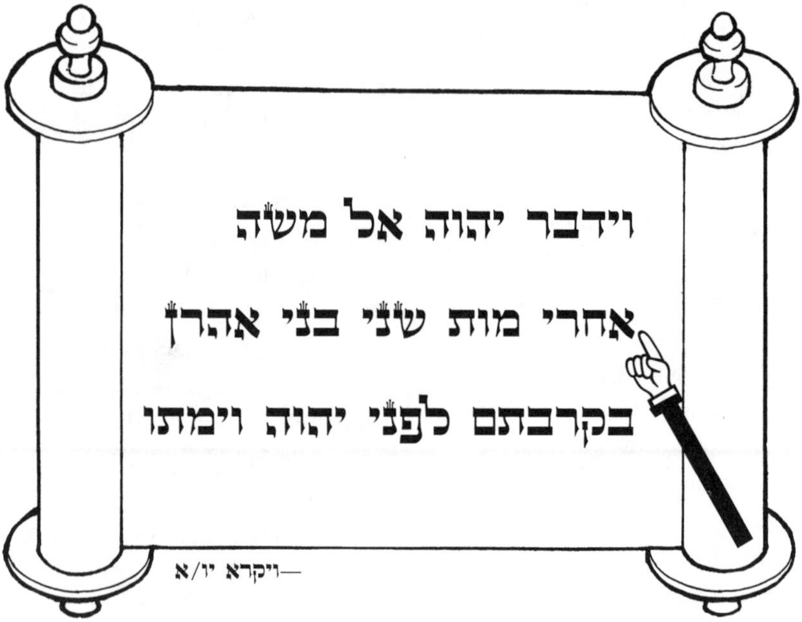

	י	רֵ	חֲ	אֲ
letter:	yod	reish	chet	alef
sound:	EE	**Rei**	CHah	(silent)-ah

	ת	וֹ	מ
letter:	tav	vav	mem
sound:	T	**OH**	M

after the death = ACHAREI MOT = **אחרי מות**

The Legend

and spoke the LORD	*va-y'da**ber** ADONAI*	וַיְדַבֵּר יְהוָה
to Moses	*el-Mo**she***	אֶל־מֹשֶׁה
<u>after the death</u> of	<u>*acha**rei** **mot***</u>	אַחֲרֵי מוֹת
two of the sons of Aaron	*sh'**nei** b'**nei** Aharon*	שְׁנֵי בְּנֵי אַהֲרֹן
in coming near-their	*b'korva**tam***	בְּקָרְבָתָם
before the LORD	*lifnei-ADONAI*	לִפְנֵי־יְהוָה
and they died	*va-ya**moo**too*	וַיָּמֻתוּ׃

—Leviticus 16:1

Related Words

afterwards	***achar** kach*	אַחַר כָּךְ
afternoon	***achar** ha-tsoho**ra**yim*	אַחַר הַצָּהֳרַיִם
last, final	*acha**rone***	אַחֲרוֹן
latter prophets	*n'vi'**im** acharo**nim***	נְבִיאִים אַחֲרוֹנִים
end of days, millennium	*acha**rit** ha-ya**mim***	אַחֲרִית הַיָּמִים
angel of death	***mal'**ach ha-**ma**vet*	מַלְאַךְ הַמָּוֶת
death sentence	*mish**paht** **ma**vet*	מִשְׁפַּט מָוֶת
put to a violent death by God's hand	*mot ya**moot***	מוֹת יָמוּת

(Ex. 16:3, 21:12, 15-17; Lev. 20:2, 9, 10-13, 15-16, 27; 1 Ki. 2:37, 42; 1 Sam. 14:39, 44; 22:16)

Hit the Trail!

Be Holy or Die!

"* ADONAI *spoke with Moshe after the death of Aharon's two sons, when they tried to sacrifice before* ADONAI *and died . . . "

—Leviticus 16:1

Unauthorized entry! Corpse contamination defiles the holy place. God speaks directly to Moshe issuing commands to <u>restrict</u> priestly access to the Tent and the Holy of Holies. Lev. 16 is Torah's sole chapter describing the Yom Kippur liturgy for purifying the nation's sins.

ADONAI restricts access, lest the unholy perish in flames.

The narrative resumes from Lev. 10, ACHAREI MOT (*after the death of*) Nadav and Avihu. Parenthetical remarks in Lev. 11-15, TAZRIA (*she bears seed*) and M'TSORA (*infected one*), detail commands required to maintain purity or restrict impurity, respectively.

To set up the priesthood, God speaks directly to Moshe from the cloud over the ark covering (Lev. 16:2; Ex. 25:22; Num. 7:89). As at Sinai, Moshe alone enters the divine space and speaks directly to God (Dt. 5:4-5). What Moshe initiates informally, the Kohen Gadol will do formally. Once a year on Yom Kippur, he will stand before God to seek atonement for the nation's sins.

? Why were Aharon's eldest sons cut off? for burning strange incense? for entering a forbidden area? for seeing God? "For in a cloud, I make-myself seen, over the Purgation-Cover" (Fox, Lev. 16:2). Read Lev. 10:1-4; Num. 26:61.

Cleanse the Sanctuary

" Then he is to go out to the altar that is before ADONAI and make atonement for it; he is to take . . . the bull's blood and . . . the goat's blood and put it on all the horns of the altar. " —Leviticus 16:18

Uncleanness from sins of omission piles up on the altar as a result of inadvertent priestly transgressions, such as entering the Tent or eating priestly offerings in a tamei (*impure*) state.

The mercy seat and altars must be cleansed yearly from sins of omission.

Of great significance is the sprinkling of blood upon the altar, to forestall judgment for inadvertent sins. The blood of bulls and goats, which the Kohen Gadol (*High Priest*) applies to the mercy seat and the horns of the altars (Lev. 16:14, 18) at the Yom Kippur service, atones for inadvertent sins and sins of omission. The Mishnah [Yoma 3-7] expands in detail on the blood sprinkling rites of Yom Kippur (Lev. 16:6-34).

The purpose of this blood sprinkling rite of purification is to kipper (*atone for, expiate, purge*) the altar, so God will continue to dwell in the midst of His people. The nation's sins are transferred to a goat who is driven from the camp to run free in the wilderness.

***?** Notice that the two goats, designated "for Adonai" and "for Azazel," are one sin offering (Lev. 16:5). Which goat dies and which goat runs free? Explain why the one goat runs free and is not killed in the wilderness.*

Purge Impurities

"He is to make the fat of the sin offering go up in smoke on the altar."

—Leviticus 16:25

Denouement! Following sacrifice for atonement, priests pick up the loose ends: burning the fat; scrubbing the clothes and body of the man who drove Azazel from the camp; and disposing of the skin, flesh, and entrails of the bull and goats sacrificed (Lev. 16:25-27).

Removing impurities restores purity.

One might expect the chatta't (*purification*) to be completed before the olah (*ascent*) is dedicated (Lev. 16:24). Burning the fat on the altar completes the chatta't (Lev. 16:25). Yet burning the fat actually occurs after the olah is dedicated (Lev. 16:24). Finally, the Kohen Gadol declares, "Tit'haru (*you shall become pure*)" (Lev. 16:30).

The Yom Kippur liturgy does not restore holiness to the camp; it restores purity. Holiness, being set apart for God, is a state; purity is a condition which is subject to change. Declaring the camp tahor (*pure*) restores purity, a condition necessary for a holy God in a holy camp.

***?** M. Zev. 10:2 gives the rabbinic rule that the blood rite appeases, but burning the olah precedes the fat of the sin offering. Explain why blood on the altar is sufficient to purify a holy priest so he can approach God in intercession.*

Consecrate Blood

> ❝ *Adonai said to Moshe, "Speak to Aharon and his sons and to all the people of Isra'el. Tell them that this is what Adonai has ordered . . ." ❞*
>
> *—Leviticus 17:1-2*

At Sinai, God acquires worshippers to dwell around His holy abode. Because God is holy, He demands holiness from those set free from Pharaoh's yoke. Avodah (*worship, service*) to God replaces avodah (*servile labor*) to Pharaoh.

In the wilderness, eat only holy sacrifices.

To prevent sacrifices to demons in the open fields, God mandates that zevachim (*slaughter-offerings*) be offered at the door of the Ohel Mo'ed (*Tent of Meeting*) (Lev. 17:6-7).

Moshe commands Yisra'el to present all zevachim (oxen, lambs, goats) to the priests, who consecrate animal slaughter by dashing the blood and burning the fat on God's altar (Lev. 17:3-6). Torah proscribes eating blood (Lev. 17:3-4, 10-14).

In this way, respect for the sanctity of life is built into consumption. Every household ceases to eat as the unclean predators do, tearing their prey and scattering blood on the open fields. Only sh'lamim (*fellowship sacrifices*) are fit to eat in the wilderness.

? ***Recall Ex. 24:4-11. Moshe builds an altar and presents zevachim. Next, the priests and elders ascend Sinai part way, to share a covenant feast before the Lord. Explain how every household in the wilderness reenacts this feast.***

Sanctify Life

". . . When someone . . . offers a burnt offering or sacrifice without bringing it to the entrance of the tent of meeting to sacrifice it to ADONAI, that person is to be cut off from his people." —Lev. 17:8-9

All sacrifices must be brought to the door of the Ohel Mo'ed (*Tent of Meeting*). All Yisra'el feasts together on sh'lamim (*well-being sacrifices*) (Lev. 17:5). The one who fails to sacrifice at the Tent is judged a dam shafach (*shedder of blood*), whose life will be cut short!

Blood is holy, even animal blood.

"Karet (*cutting short*)" refers to an early death, or to loss of heirs, or even to loss of one's share in the world to come. Cutting off the man, and not the nefesh (*soul*), may indicate a shorter life, rather than a loss of heirs (Lev. 17:9).

Scripture assigns blood, as the carrier of life, a sacred place in the life of the community. Ritual procedures require priests to handle blood most carefully at the altar (Lev. 17:6). Strict prohibitions on the eating of blood apply to the citizen and ger (*sojourner*) alike. Six times (Lev. 17:3-4, 10-14), Torah prohibits eating blood! This prohibition extends into the New Covenant (Acts 15:29).

***?** Only a life on the altar of God can atone for the human soul. Study Lev. 17:11, Jn. 6:54-60. What is hard about Yeshua's teaching? Explain how eating the "body" and "blood" of Yeshua is the soul's covenant meal of eternal life.*

Sanctify Family

> ❝ *None of you is to approach anyone who is a close relative in order to have sexual relations; I am* ADONAI. ❞
>
> *—Leviticus 18:6*

Immediate family, called sh'erim (*flesh relations*), are off-limits for sexual partners. These include all persons who are in-house: parents, stepmother, sister, grandchildren, half-sister, aunt, uncle's wife, daughter-in-law, and sister-in-law (Lev. 18:7-16).

Forbidden relationships make God's camp impure.

With such persons under the same roof, one needn't go out to the streets l'galot ervah (*to uncover nakedness*), the first part of the sexual act [Ramban on Lev. 20:17; cf. Gen. 9:22-23].

A second forbidden class of sexual partners describes persons in affinal relationship [Levine, p. 255]: related kin such as mother and daughter, a woman and her sister, a niddah (*menstruant*), and a neighbor's wife (Lev. 18:17-20).

Finally, Torah speaks to the most immoral of all relationships, dedicating or sacrificing children to Molech (Lev. 18:21). Forbidden relations make God's house impure, driving Him from His own household, the camp.

? ***Read 1 Cor. 11:3, 3:21-23. In the New Covenant as in the Old, God heads His household. Does Eph. 2:19 address Jews and gentiles as co-equals in the house of Yeshua? Is male headship anachronistic or part of God's order? Explain.***

Safeguard the House

> *“You are not to go to bed with a man as with a woman; it is an abomination.”*
>
> *—Leviticus 18:22*

Prohibitions relating to non-child-producing relationships constitute the present segment. Torah labels sexual relationships outside of households as abominations! These include homosexuality and bestiality.

The Land cannot tolerate abominations.

The prohibitions are binding on both the citizen and the ger, whether *proselyte* [Sifra] or *sojourner* [Ibn Ezra]. God descended to destroy Sodom for its abominations (Gen. 19).

God holds men, as heads of households, directly accountable for such sins (Lev. 18:23a addresses men in the second person; Lev. 18:23b addresses women in the less direct, third person).

Whether the act of “wasted seed” or the violation of boundaries between man and animal, such a practice is classified as to’evah (*an abomination*). The Land, personified as a life force, becomes tamei (*impure*) and “will vomit out” the Canaanites for such abominable practices (Lev. 18:24-27).

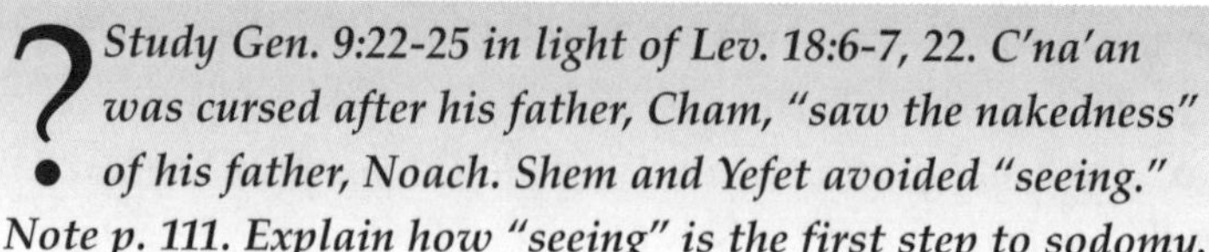

? *Study Gen. 9:22-25 in light of Lev. 18:6-7, 22. C’na’an was cursed after his father, Cham, “saw the nakedness” of his father, Noach. Shem and Yefet avoided “seeing.” Note p. 111. Explain how “seeing” is the first step to sodomy.*

Safeguard the Camp

> *“So keep my charge not to follow any of these abominable customs that others before you have followed and thus defile yourselves by doing them. I am ADONAI your God.”* —*Leviticus 18:30*

Perverting sexuality in ways that do not produce children is called "to'evah (*an abomination*)." The practice appears five times in the shvi'i section (Lev. 18:22, 26, 27, 29, 30).

The land vomits out the camp that tolerates abominations within it.

"To'evah" appears only once more in Leviticus—in the next parashah, where we're called to be K'DOSHIM (*holy ones*). Torah prescribes the death penalty for men who commit sodomy (Lev. 20:13).

God compares the holiness of marriage directly with the covenant relationship to Himself—beginning and ending the chapter with "I am ADONAI your God" (Lev. 18:1, 30). He expels the Canaanites from the land on account of unholy, abominable relationships.

Scripture poetically personifies the Land as a living creature that violently rejects food it detests. The Land "vomits out" the unclean inhabitants who defile themselves (Lev. 18:25-30), whether the sons of C'na'an or the sons of Yisra'el.

***?** It is politically incorrect today to call homosexual relationships an abomination punishable by death. Only the Land of C'na'an "vomits out" those who defile it in this way. Explain the New Covenant view (Eph. 5:5-6; Ro. 1:24-32).*

Sanctify the City *Meander*

> ***"I will scatter you . . . thus I will remove your defilement . . . and you will cause yourselves to be profaned in full view of the Goyim. Then you will know that I am ADONAI.'" —Ezekiel 22:15-16***

Eight times, Y'chezkel (*Ezekiel*) chastises Yisra'el for violating holy prohibitions regarding blood. The people have been debased to bloodsuckers in all areas of life. As a result, God personally shortens the community's length of days in the Land.

> ***God cuts short life in the Land, to cleanse Yisra'el.***

Y'hudah has become a "city of blood" (Ez. 22:2). Their sins include child sacrifices during M'nasheh's reign (v. 2), Bacchanalian orgies or open idolatry (v. 9), bloodshed (vv. 2-4, 6, 9, 12), and forbidden relationships which uncover their father's nakedness (vv. 10-11, cf. Lev. 18:7).

Having succumbed to incest, bestiality, and child sacrifice, Yisra'el is judged by God (Ez. 22:4). In captivity among the nations, she is "profaned in full view of the *Goyim*" (Ez. 22:15-16). But all is not lost. At Y'rushalayim, the siege commences as fires purify the nation (Ez. 22:16-22; 23:25-27). Never again will Yisra'el collectively approve of child sacrifices to a foreigner's idol!

? *Yisra'el's national life gives way to utter carnality. To renew His people, God exiles them from the Land. Read Heb. 12:11 and 2 Cor. 4:16-18. When your holiness is overcome, explain what steps you take to renew yourself.*

Sanctify the Kingdom

> *" . . . for you were bought at a price. So use your bodies to glorify God. "*
>
> *—1 Corinthians 6:20*

Greeks viewed the body and the material order as headed for destruction. Only the soul was immortal. The Corinthians thought the body stood for nothing. As a result, sexual matters were transitory and unimportant.

Believers' bodies house the Ruach haKodesh.

Porneia (*illicit sex*) was widespread in Corinth (1 Cor. 6:9; 7:2; 2 Cor. 12:21) and condoned by public opinion in Greece and Rome. In fact, the Greek Christians at Corinth attacked Paul for his Jewish worldview!

Rav Sha'ul stated that the believer was "bought at a price," much in the same way as purchasing a slave at market (1 Cor. 7:23; Ro. 6:17). With the change in ownership, believers lack freedom to practice porneia (i.e. join themselves with prostitutes, cf. 1 Cor. 6:16). Rather, sexual matters fit into an abiding, life-creating moral order. The fallen order will be redeemed and made whole. The body must be treated as holy, the temple of the living God (1 Cor. 6:19).

? Compare 1 Cor. 6:18 with Lev. 18:8, 10. Note that bodily sin radiates impurity upon heads of households. Explain how a life of gross carnality can drive out the Ruach haKodesh from dwelling in the temple of an impure believer.

Talk Your Walk . . .

Acharei Mot (*after the death*) of Aharon's sons, the Lord restricts access to the Holy of Holies. Only on Yom Kippur does the anointed Kohen Gadol, washed and clothed in white, enter God's Presence. He averts his glance from looking upon the divine Presence, lest he see God and die! Each year, the sanctuary and the nation must be cleansed of all sins, transgressions, and iniquities.

Purity is restored when contagious and infectious impurities are removed from the camp. The Kohen Gadol enters the Holy of Holies to stand before God's footstool. Upon the kapporet (*gold cover of the ark, the seat of mercy*), he sprinkles the blood of bulls and goats, to make atonement for himself, his household, and the nation.

God commands that His house be purified from year to year.

God orders all sacrifices to be brought to the sanctuary, so that His people do not act as predators, leaving blood uncovered on open fields. The unauthorized shedding of blood is treated as murder. In like manner, forbidden relationships mix blood in ways that pollute households. Blood is holy, the actual carrier of life. Whereas the sacred use of blood can cleanse the nation, the unholy use of blood defiles the nation.

The Land cannot tolerate an impure people. Too much impurity will drive God from the camp. Then the Lord will order the Land to "vomit out" a people who have defiled themselves with abominations.

Oasis

. . . Walk Your Talk

Ponder the complexity of the ritual process on the High Holy Day of Yom Kippur. The Kohen Gadol (*High Priest*) completely immerses himself with exceptional care in his duties of the day. He attends to fifteen sacrificial offerings including the two goats for Adonai and Azazel, three incense offerings, five changes of garments, five immersions in mikveh, vidui (*confession*) three times, ten hand washings, 43 sprinklings of blood, and four prayers saying aloud the ineffable Tetragrammaton, יְהוָה.

Yeshua has told us that unless our righteousness surpasses that of the scribes and Pharisees, we cannot enter the Kingdom of Heaven. Yet works of righteousness pursued zealously with all our might will fall short. What can be done? How does one translate the righteousness that comes by faith into holy behaviors that exceed the righteousness of those who were the community's anointed gatekeepers?

> ***Spirit-filled prayer enables believer-priests to abide in holiness.***

Do you spend time and energy rigorously attending to holiness in your life? Do you see yourself as a believer-priest? Do you prepare yourself daily to stand—face to face—in the awesome Presence of the LORD?

Shabbat Shalom!

"קדשים," said God,
"Be holy ones for Me!
Keep My rules and statutes,
so you will stay free.
Love your neighbor as yourself,
do it honestly.
And keep the justice!
Live in harmony!"

God set us apart
as a nation of menchen,
to help the homeless
get more than park benchen.
Uncleanness makes (Oy!)
a big problem I'll mention . . .
the land vomits out
those who make it
a stenchen!!!

Walk K'DOSHIM!
19:1-20:27

Holy ones

TORAH—Leviticus 19:1-20:27

1st Emulate the Holy One—Leviticus 19:1-2
2nd Holy Love—Leviticus 19:15
3rd Holy Fruit—Leviticus 19:23
4th Holy Sojourners—Leviticus 19:33
5th Holy Children—Leviticus 20:1-2
6th Holy Household—Leviticus 20:8
7th Holy Land—Leviticus 20:23
Maftir Holy Nation—Leviticus 20:27

HAFTARAH—Ezekiel 22:1-19; 20:2-20

Made Holy in Exile—Ezekiel 20:19-20

B'RIT CHADASHAH—Matthew 5:43-48

Like the Holy One—Matthew 5:48

Holy Ones, Stay Close to God!

Looking Back

VAYIKRA ADONAI el Moshe (*and the LORD called to Moses*), as corporate head, to draw near to the tabernacle, radiating from God's glorious Presence!

VAYIKRA *ADONAI*
from the Tent and tells Moshe,
TSAV *the priests*
to learn ritual procedures . . .
Then on day* SH'MINI, *they can
distinguish clean from unclean.

***When a woman* TAZRIA,**
she needs cleansing from childbirth.
A* M'TSORA *also needs to be clean
before re-entering the camp.

ACHAREI MOT *Aharon's sons,*
priests take care to enter
according to strict ritual procedure.
We all must strive to be
K'DOSHIM, *holy ones,*
for God is holy!

God further instructs Moshe: TSAV (*command!*) the priests to follow ritual procedures when receiving offerings from Yisra'el. Elevate the priests for holy service. Consecrate them seven days.

Then ba-yom ha-SH'MINI (on *the eighth day*), commence the service of the sanctuary. Aharon's sons, zealous to offer incense, jump ahead of orders and die in the holy place. Nobody knows what to do . . .

Scripture devotes the next two parashiot to distinguishing tahor (*pure/not impure*) from tamei (*impure/contagious*). When a woman TAZRIA (*bears seed*), she remains ritually impure for a week. On the eighth day, she can return to her husband; but she is still tamei to enter God's house or to consume offerings designated for priestly families. Instead, she must wait a total of 40 days (or 80 days from the birth of a daughter),

Log

before completing her days of filling. Then she can ascend to the altar in a pure state.

In contrast, waiting is not sufficient for the **M'TSORA** (*infected one*). He must be healed by God to become ritually cleansed. Otherwise, he is barred indefinitely from the camp and must cry out, "Tamei! Tamei!"

ACHAREI MOT (*after the death of*) Nadav and Avihu, God restricts immediate access to His holy Presence. He orders yearly cleansing of the camp on Yom Kippur to restore purity and remove impurities introduced by sin.

Respect for the sanctity of life requires all blood to be consecrated. Blood is holy, specially reserved for creating life, removing impurity, or restoring purity in the camp where the Holy One dwells.

In K'DOSHIM . . .

The Key People are Moshe (*Moses*) and the whole assembly.

The Scene is the tabernacle, in the wilderness of Sinai.

Main Events include the LORD telling Moshe to say, "Be holy because I, the LORD your God, am holy;" various laws to keep the people holy; and a list of punishments for sin.

We all are called to become **K'DOSHIM** (*holy ones*), for God is holy! He radiates holiness to the sanctuary and to the priests: Ani ADONAI m'kadish'chem (*I am the LORD Who makes you holy*), the house of Yisra'el.

But Yisra'el must obey Torah, keep the covenant, and maintain holiness—in the Land, in the households, and in the nation. In short, with help from God, Yisra'el must struggle to be holy ones . . .

The Trail Ahead 

The Path

	ם	י	שׁ	ד	קְ
letter:	mem sofeet	yod	shin	dalet	koof
sound:	M	EE	**SHee**	Doh	K’

holy ones = **K’DOSHIM** = **קדשים**

Work

The Legend

and spoke the LORD	*va-y'da**ber** ADONAI*	וַיְדַבֵּר יְהוָה
to Moses,	*el-Mo**she***	אֶל־מֹשֶׁה
saying, speak	*le**mor** da**ber***	לֵּאמֹר: דַּבֵּר
to all the congregation of	*el-kol-a**dat***	אֶל־כָּל־עֲדַת
the sons of Israel	*b'nei-Yisra'**el***	בְּנֵי־יִשְׂרָאֵל
and you will say to them	*v'amar**ta** ale**hem***	וְאָמַרְתָּ אֲלֵהֶם
holy ones you will be	*k'do**shim** tih'**yoo***	קְדֹשִׁים תִּהְיוּ
because holy am I	*ki ka**dosh** A**ni***	כִּי קָדוֹשׁ אֲנִי
the LORD God-your	*ADONAI Elohei**chem***	יְהוָה אֱלֹהֵיכֶם׃

—*Leviticus 19:1-2*

Related Words

consecrate, sanctify, dedicate	*ka**dash***	קָדַשׁ
apartness, holiness	***ko**desh*	קֹדֶשׁ
holy to the LORD	***ko**desh l'Ado**nai***	קֹדֶשׁ לְיהוָה
holy place, sanctuary	*mik**dash***	מִקְדָּשׁ
Holy of Holies	***ko**desh ha-koda**shim***	קֹדֶשׁ הַקֳּדָשִׁים
The Holy City (Jerusalem)	*'ir ha-**ko**desh*	עִיר הַקֹּדֶשׁ
Holy Spirit	*ru**ach** ha-**ko**desh*	רוּחַ הַקֹּדֶשׁ

Hit the Trail!

Emulate the Holy One

" Adonai said to Moshe, "Speak to the entire community of Isra'el; tell them, 'You people are to be holy because I, Adonai your God, am holy.'" "

—Leviticus 19:1-2

K'DOSHIM (*holy ones*) develop the kind of character that honors a holy God. Kol adat Yisra'el (*the whole community of Israel*) shares the collective responsibility to become holy, since God is holy (Lev. 19:2).

Become holy, for God is holy.

Holiness radiates [Joosten, p. 128]. Those nearest God absorb His holiness. In this way, priestly privilege extends to those in proximity to God. However, higher standards in conduct come with the territory. Thus eating food that is n'veilah (*died on its own/not ritually slaughtered*) or t'reifah (*torn*), for example, is permitted for the ger toshav (*resident-settler*), but not for Yisra'el (Lev. 22:8; Dt. 14:21).

Holiness is more than a quality or power; it has relational and experiential meaning, enacted and actualized in the life of community [Gorman, p.111]. All Yisra'el must tira'u (*hold in awe*) their parents as co-creators of life, keep Shabbat as holy, and respect the downtrodden—society's poor, deaf, and blind.

? ***Compare Lev. 19:14 with Ro. 11:10-11. Holiness requires that one never place a stumbling block in front of the blind. Rav Sha'ul asks if blind Yisra'el has stumbled so as to fall. Answer this question in light of Lev. 19:14.***

Holy Love

> *❝ Do not be unjust in judging—show neither partiality to the poor nor deference to the mighty, but with justice judge your neighbor. ❞*
>
> *—Leviticus 19:15*

Judgments must not be influenced by a person's status. Just judges show no partiality for the poor, nor favoritism for the great. One's neighbor must be judged with equity and even-handedness (Lev. 19:15). ". . . in righteousness shall you judge your neighbor" [Sifra, p. 107].

Practice godly judgment: love your neighbor.

The emphasis on judgment forms the context for loving your neighbor as yourself (Lev. 19:18, cf. Mk. 12:31-33). One must neither "take-vengeance" nor "retain-anger" against an Israelite or a ger (*sojourner*) (Fox, Lev. 19:18, 34).

Talmud tells the story of a man who accidentally chopped off his own hand while cutting meat. Says Munk, "No one would imagine that he would be tempted to take revenge upon his right hand for having cut off his left" (p. 221). Nursing hatred, whether actively (as a desire for vengeance) or passively (in bearing a grudge), is both an unloving and ungodly way to judge!

? *Study Lev. 19:17-18. How can you avoid "bearing the sins" of your neighbor? If your neighbor sins, under what circumstances is gentle reproof the loving thing to do? How is holy love willing to rebuke one's neighbor as oneself?*

Holy Fruit

> ❝ *When you enter the land and plant various kinds of fruit trees, you are to regard its fruit as forbidden—for three years it will be forbidden to you and not eaten.* ❞
> —*Leviticus 19:23*

Holy people, called to sanctify and redeem the Land, must obey God by not eating fruit from a forbidden tree.

Firstfruits of a newly planted tree are considered unfit and must not be eaten for the first three years. This fruit is referred to as "orlah (lit. *uncircumcision*)," unfit like a foreskin (Fox, Lev. 19:23).

Fourth year fruit is kodesh hilulim l'ADONAI (*holy of praise to ADONAI*). Considered second tithe, all the fruit is picked, carried up to Y'rushalayim, and eaten before God amidst praise and thanksgiving [Sifra, Rashi]. The fifth year, the fruit may be eaten. It is no longer classified as orlah.

Sanctify fruit as holy in the Holy Land.

Practicing the mitzvah of orlah weans people from selfishness. By devoting the fruit exclusively to God's praise and service, one learns the lessons of prosperity [*Ma'or v'Shamesh*]. In this way, the creation is redeemed. Obeying Torah redeems eating fruit from the forbidden tree!

? *Read Lev. 25:23. The underlying assumption of orlah (and all restrictions on harvests in the Land) is that the owner of the soil has the status of "steward," not owner. Who actually owns the Land? Who owns the Land today?*

Holy Sojourners

"If a foreigner stays with you in your land, do not do him wrong."

—Leviticus 19:33

Ger! *Proselyte?* [Rashi, Rambam, Sifra, Stone] or *foreigner?* [Sforno, Stern, Wenham, Joosten]. Rambam sees the verse above as a special command to love the proselyte [Hil. De'os 6:4]. It is forbidden to taunt a non-Jew, saying that his past renders him unfit for Torah study [Rashi, Sifra].

Grant the landless the privilege to sojourn.

In contrast, others see a comparison to the Exodus experience. As sojourners in Egypt, the sons of Yisra'el understood the hurt felt by the unwanted stranger. Thus, Yisra'el must love the stranger (cf. Ex. 22:21(20תנ"ך); 23:9; Dt. 10:19) and remember her past as gerim (*sojourners*) in Egypt (Gen. 15:13; 47:4; Dt. 26:5).

Since the landless are downtrodden and dependent upon the goodwill of the inhabitants of the Land, the foreigner who has settled in the Land must be granted the right to stay [Joosten, p. 61]. In this way, the ger is loved as a fellow Israelite (Lev. 19:34, 18).

***?** Recall that Avraham was a landless sojourner (Gen. 23:4), and the sons of Yisra'el remain stewards of God's land today (Lev. 25:23). Discuss shared experiences of Avraham, Yisra'el, and believers in Yeshua as sojourners today.*

Holy Children

❝ *ADONAI said to Moshe, "Say to the people of Isra'el, 'If someone . . . sacrifices one of his children to Molekh . . . the people of the land are to stone him to death.'"* ❞ *—Leviticus 20:1-2*

Am haAretz (*the people of the Land*) must stone anyone bringing outright defilement upon God's dwelling (Lev. 20:3).

Molech worship must be wiped out!

Molech worship is so toxic that it defiles the sanctuary from afar. Impurities pollute, driving God from dwelling in the camp. The people must condemn and punish those who dedicate children to this idol (Lev. 20:3a; 18:21). If the community fails to impose capital punishment, then God will impose karet (*cutting off*) of the seed (Lev. 20:4-5).

Note that the holy and the impure are contagious states that do not mix [Milgrom, pp. 729-732]. In contrast, chol (*common*) and tahor (*pure*) states cannot spread by contact. Objects can be both common and pure, or both holy and pure, or even common and impure. But mixing the kadosh (*holy*) and the tamei (*impure*) is explosive! Molech worship in the tabernacle makes nitroglycerin look tame by comparison.

? ***Both holiness and impurity have a leavening effect. Holiness radiates, elevates, and renders holy; impurities pollute and defile. (Compare Mt. 13:33 with Lk. 12:1). Describe the contagious effect of the holy and the impure.***

Holy Household

“ Observe my regulations, and obey them; I am Adonai, who sets you apart to be holy. ”
—Leviticus 20:8

Safeguarding the holiness of the tabernacle, God’s house, dominates the world of Leviticus. Yisra’el must purify its house, because a holy God demands a holy house: I am the Lord, m’kadish’chem (*the one-who-hallows you!*) (Fox, Lev. 20:8)

Members of a household must be holy to the head.

Those who curse father or mother attack the head of the house and must be put to death (Lev. 20:9). Lying with the father’s wife insults the honor of the father as head of the house (Lev. 20:11). Sleeping with conjugal relatives in your father’s house is an offense against yourself; and in your brother’s house, an offense against your brother (Lev. 20:19, 21).

Finally, Torah enjoins the nation to stone any citizen or ger (*sojourner*) who sacrifices his child to Molech; the practice is an abomination (Lev. 20:2). Thus, holiness within God’s household imposes requirements on all persons residing in His house, even on the ger (*resident alien*).

? God says Molech worshippers “prostitute themselves,” committing spiritual adultery against His house. Study Lev. 20:5, Jn. 8:1-11. In terms of strict justice and mercy, explain how Yeshua maintains the holiness of God’s house.

Holy Land

“ Do not live by the regulations of the nation which I am expelling ahead of you; because they did all these things, which is why I detested them. ”
—Leviticus 20:23

Failure to obey statutes and ordinances defiles the Land and results in expulsion (Lev. 20:8, 22). The Land cannot tolerate immorality (Lev. 18:26-30). "Thus the gift of the Land is conditioned upon the people maintaining their high level of sanctity" [Stone, p. 670, n22-24].

Those who defile the Land will be cut off!

Blessing in the Land flows from the holiness of God's people in keeping the covenant. Canaanite practices included idolatry and sexual license already proscribed (Ex. 23:23-24; Lev. 20:9-22). The curse upon C'na'an can be traced to a most unusual reference to Cham as "the father of" C'na'an, along with his participation in uncovering the nakedness of Noach, Cham's father (Gen. 9:22; Lev. 20:11). Indeed, the basis for God's driving out Canaanites from the Land is rooted in karet (*cutting off* the seed). God personally undertook to drive out the fertility cult of the Canaanite tribes (Lev. 20:23). Beware their customs, warns God.

? Read Lev. 20:23-24, the whole of the shvi'i segment excluding the maftir! In verse 23, God Himself drives out the Canaanites to cleanse the Land of abominations. Explain why God cuts off the house of C'na'an.

Holy Nation

> ***"A man or a woman who is a spirit-medium or sorcerer must be put to death; they are to stone them to death; their blood will be on them."***
> ***—Leviticus 20:27***

Instructions to separate pure animals from tamei (*impure*) animals concludes the maftir (Lev. 20:25). The next verse gives the reason: "Rather, you people are to be holy [*K'DOSHIM*] for me; because I, ADONAI, am holy; and I have set you apart from the other peoples, so that you can belong to me" (Lev. 20:26).

> ***Yisra'el is to be holy, a nation set apart for God.***

God separates Yisra'el from among the nations. Yisra'el's dietary laws conform to the statutes and ordinances that maintain the nation's separation from other nations (Lev. 11). Yisra'el must be holy by distinguishing clean from unclean animals. Priests and prophets—not spirit-mediums—call the nation to holy behaviors legislated in Torah.

Torah cuts off all spirit-mediums and sorcerers, as sources of impurity which neither the Land nor God can tolerate. Torah prescribes death by stoning for divination, because d'meihem bam (*their blood is on them*) (Lev. 20:27).

? ***In a theocracy, spirit-mediums must die. In a secular society, the wheat and tares grow alongside one another. Read Matthew 13:37-43. Explain whether or not spirit-mediums in the church are guilty of capital offenses.***

Made Holy in Exile *Meander*

***"** I am ADONAI your God; live by my laws . . . and keep my shabbats holy; and they will be a sign between me and you, so that you will know that I am ADONAI your God. **"** —Ezekiel 20:19-20*

Zadokites ruled as High Priests from the time of David to the Hasmoneans. Zadok sided with David at the Absalom rebellion (2 Sam. 19:11(12תנ"ך)). Now yet another Zadokite preaches to those facing exile from Y'rushalayim.

God sends a Zadokite to restore the priestly nation.

Y'chezkel (*Ezekiel*) warns his generation not to live by the rules and customs of their parents, but rather to shed their idolatries (Ez. 20:18). According to a standard of strict justice, the nation should perish for following Egyptian statutes [Ez. 20:7-8; Josh. 24:14; Soncino, p. 122].

A pattern unfolds. Yisra'el rejects God's rules and desecrates His Shabbats (Ez. 20:13). Yisra'el's disobedience defames God's name and hinders His efforts to redeem the nations (Ez. 20:9, 14); yet in grace, He continues to extend compassion (Ez. 20:17) and resists finishing them off. What began during the exodus continues in the exile.

? *Read Ez. 20:16-17, cf. Ro. 10:19. Explain why God does not annihilate Yisra'el. What is the basis for God's compassion upon disobedient Yisra'el, especially since Yisra'el's actions frustrate God's plan to reach the nations?*

Like the Holy One

> *“Therefore, be perfect, just as your Father in heaven is perfect.”*
>
> *—Matthew 5:48*

Holiness includes being loving in godly ways!

Be perfectly loving!

Yeshua set the standards for His talmidim (*students*) when he said, "unless your righteousness is far greater than that of the *Torah*-teachers and *P'rushim*, you will certainly not enter the Kingdom of Heaven" (Mt. 5:20)!

Yeshua extends the standard of love for one's neighbor and for the ger (*sojourner*) to one's enemies too! Application of a principle of strict justice (apart from mercy) would have destroyed Yisra'el for practicing idolatry in the wilderness (Ez. 20:18).

Now, Rav Sha'ul calls upon the gentiles to show unconditional love to Yisra'el—even when Yisra'el manifestly opposes God's plan to redeem the nations (Ro. 11:28). In striking contrast to Yisra'el, God shows love to the nations when they are in disobedience (Ro. 11:30). He calls gentiles to emulate His holy love to Yisra'el and to perfect that love (Mt. 5:48).

? Read Mt. 5:45, Ro. 12:21. The Father who bestows sun and rain on the righteous and the unrighteous alike now calls New Covenant believers to extend love to those who love us not. How does one overcome evil with good?

Talk Your Walk . . .

God calls the whole community of Yisra'el to become holy. Individuals must walk the path of holiness, because God is holy. Since God dwells in the midst of the camp, He radiates holiness throughout the camp. The people must respect the laws and ordinances. Firstfruits must be set aside for God, for the kohanim, and for the place where God will choose to dwell in the Land.

God's camp is holy, too. Those who surround him—including sojourners—must respect and observe certain rules in the community. In turn, Yisra'el must not favor the strong or oppress the weak.

Molech worship and other idolatrous practices must be stamped out. Individuals must keep themselves pure when entering the sanctuary of the LORD. Moreover, all Yisra'el, in covenant with God, must worship God alone and stay holy to Him.

Requirements for God's house extend, by analogy, to the households of the community. The head of the house must be treated with respect. Unholy behaviors such as adultery are treated in a manner similar to idolatry. Those who practice such deeds are summarily cut off from community, and even stoned! The Land cannot tolerate immorality; indeed, the entire community can be "barfed out," exiled and cut off. The nation must remain holy, in covenant to God.

Become holy by belonging to God.

Oasis

. . . Walk Your Talk

Wouldn't it be nice if holiness were some kind of button that we could push once, and then it just happened? We might push the button with great fear and trepidation, but then the struggle for holiness would be over!

Alas, things are not quite so simple. Torah tells us, ". . . you are to hallow-yourselves" (Fox, Lev. 20:7a). The B'rit Chadashah commands, ". . . be perfect, just as your Father in heaven is perfect" (Mt. 5:48). Yet we also are told ADONAI is "the one-who-hallows-you" (Fox, Lev. 20:8b). Holiness requires us to struggle, with the knowledge that divine assistance will fill in the gaps that our human weaknesses necessarily create.

Struggle for holiness!

With failure as a given, try we must! Yet trying harder does not really guarantee success. A secret operates—prayer changes things, as does the opportunity to renew amidst failure. Spending time in God's Presence invites God's holiness to transform our inner man. As will become clear in the next portion, however, those nearest God are subject to ever stricter standards—guaranteeing greater gaps and a new cycle of prayer, renewal, and time in God's Presence. Are you ready to try again?

Shabbat Shalom!

אמר means "Say!"
as in "Say to the priests,
'Stay clean for the LORD!
Don't touch dead beasts!
Eat kosher food
at all of your feasts.
Give barley firstfruits
before eating wheats!'"

For right in your midst
the Holy One dwells.
Think hard on this marvel
until it gels.
Stop blasphemy cold,
stone the guy who rebels.
With zeal clean your camp!
Do all Torah tells!

Walk Emor!
21:1-24:23

Say!

Torah—Leviticus 21:1-24:23

1st Words for Kohanim—Leviticus 21:1-2a
2nd Drawing Near—Leviticus 21:16-17
3rd Gifts for God—Leviticus 22:17-19
4th Proclaiming Holy Times—Leviticus 23:1-2
5th Time to Repent—Leviticus 23:23-24
6th Time to Rejoice—Leviticus 23:33-34
7th Feasting on Holiness—Leviticus 24:1-2
Maftir Keeping the Camp Pure—Leviticus 24:23

Haftarah—Ezekiel 44:15-31

Holy Living—Ezekiel 44:31

B'rit Chadashah—Luke 14:12-24

Feasting at God's Banquet—Luke 14:24

Say to the Priests, "Be Holy to God!"

 Looking Back

VAYIKRA ADONAI el Moshe (*and the LORD called to Moses*), to draw near to His glorious Presence in the tabernacle.

> ***VAYIKRA** the LORD from the Tent. He tells Moshe, **TSAV** the priests so they can begin their service on day **SH'MINI**.*
>
> *A woman who **TAZRIA** and the **M'TSORA** must both be ritually cleansed before approaching God. **ACHAREI MOT** two priests bearing strange fire, everyone follows strict ritual procedures.*
>
> *To emulate God, we must become **K'DOSHIM**. The LORD sets higher standards for some. He orders Moshe, "**EMOR**—say to the priests . . . "*

God further instructs Moshe: TSAV (*command!*) the priests to receive offerings from Yisra'el. Take seven days to consecrate these men.

Ba-yom ha-SH'MINI (*on the eighth day*), the priests begin serving in the sanctuary. But things go wrong! Zealous to offer incense, Nadav and Avihu jump ahead of orders and die in the holy place . . .

The next two parashiot stress the importance of being tahor (*pure/not impure*). When a woman TAZRIA (*bears seed*), she remains tamei (*impure*) after childbirth. Only after waiting a set time can she approach the altar in a pure state. Waiting is not enough for the M'TSORA (*infected one*). Unless God heals him, he remains barred indefinitely from the camp.

ACHAREI MOT (*after the death of*) Aharon's two sons, God restricts access to His

Log

holy Presence. He orders the camp cleansed every Yom Kippur to restore purity lost by sin.

Respect for the sanctity of life requires all blood to be consecrated. Blood is holy, specially reserved for creating life, removing impurity, or restoring purity in the camp where the Holy One dwells.

All Yisra'el must obey Torah, keep the covenant, and maintain holiness—in the Land, in the households, and in the nation. In short, with help from God, we all must strive to become **K'DOSHIM** (*holy ones*), for *He* is holy!

But God requires an even higher standard of holiness from the priests. He tells Moshe: **EMOR** (*say!*) to the priests . . .

In EMOR . . .

The Key People are Moshe (*Moses*), the sons of Aharon (*Aaron*), and Aharon (*Aaron*).

The Scene is the tabernacle, in the wilderness of Sinai.

Main Events include the LORD giving Moshe rules for priests to stay holy, with special rules for the high priest; guidelines for treating the sacred offerings with respect, including what may be eaten by whom and which animals are acceptable as sacrifices; descriptions of the appointed feasts to proclaim as sacred assemblies, including Shabbat, Pesach and the Feast of Unleavened Bread, Firstfruits, Shavu'ot, Rosh haShanah, Yom Kippur, Sukkot, and Sh'mini Atseret; instructions for the priests to tend the lamps and bake bread to set before the Lord; and the story of a blasphemer stoned as the Lord commanded; guidelines for restitution—life for life.

The Trail Ahead

The Path

	ר	מֹ	אֱ
letter:	reish	mem	alef
sound:	R	**Moh**	(silent)-eh

say! = EMOR = **אמר**

Work

The Legend

and said the LORD	*va-**yo**mer* ADONAI	וַיֹּאמֶר יְהוָה
to Moses,	*el-Mo**she***	אֶל־מֹשֶׁה
say	***emor***	אֱמֹר
to the priests,	*el-ha-koha**nim***	אֶל־הַכֹּהֲנִים
sons of Aaron,	*b'**nei** Aha**ron***	בְּנֵי אַהֲרֹן
and you will say to them	*v'amar**ta** ale**hem***	וְאָמַרְתָּ אֲלֵהֶם
for a [dead] soul	*l'**ne**fesh*	לְנֶפֶשׁ
not will unclean oneself	*lo-yita**ma***	לֹא־יִטַּמָּא
among people-his	*b'a**mav***	בְּעַמָּיו׃

—*Leviticus 21:1*

Related Words

say, tell, utter, name	*a**mar***	אָמַר
words (Gen. 49:21)	***ei**mer*	אֵמֶר
it is said (rumored that)	*om'**rim***	אוֹמְרִים
how do you say __?	*eich om'**rim**?*	אֵיך אוֹמְרִים?
that is to say, in other words	*k'lo**mar***	כְּלוֹמַר

Hit the Trail!

Words for Kohanim

“ ADONAI said to Moshe, "Speak to the cohanim, the sons of Aharon; tell them: 'No cohen is to make himself unclean for any of his people who dies, except for his close relatives . . . '" ” —Lev. 21:1-2a

More than a double standard for leadership, standards of holiness rise as those around the LORD move closer to Him. Kohanim observe higher standards than for laity or Levites, and the Kohen Gadol observes the highest standards of all!

Perfect holiness means fitting into God's picture.

Being sanctified means becoming fit to be with the LORD. In the case of priests, failure to observe priestly commands (e.g., on mourning and marriage) can profane the sanctuary (Lev. 21:6). Kohanim may only mourn the loss of sh'erim (*close family relations*): mother, father, brother, son, daughter, and virgin sister (Lev. 21:1-7; cf. Lev. 21:12). Kohanim can marry only a virgin or the widow of a priest, but not a divorcee or a prostitute (Lev. 21:7).

Holy behaviors may sound discriminatory to western ears. But what is kosher (*fit*) does not carry good or bad connotations in the Semitic world. As in constructing a puzzle, each fit helps to complete the whole!

? *Study Lev. 21:10-15. Explain why the Kohen Gadol may not mourn the death of a sh'er (flesh relation). Why does leaving the sanctuary profane it? How does a properly clothed priest on duty radiate God's holiness to the nation?*

Drawing Near

“ Adonai said to Moshe, “Tell Aharon, ‘None of your descendants who has a defect may approach to offer the bread of his God.’” ”

—Leviticus 21:16-17

Blemished priests, as blemished sacrifices, are not permitted to draw near to the altar or minister in the holy place, receiving offerings from the people, either kodshei kodashim (*most holy*) or even kodashim (*holy*).

Drawing near to God requires perfection.

Blemished priests include the blind, lame, mutilated, broken-limbed, or those with skin, eye, and genital deformities. Anything that mars the perfection (wholeness) of the kohen excludes him from officiating; however, penalties for officiating are relatively light [Munk, p. 260]. In fact, priests with blemishes can eat holy sacrifices.

In contrast, eating holy offerings in a tamei (*impure*) state—especially knowingly—incurs severe punishment, either mitah bidei shamayim (*death by the hand of heaven*) or karet (*cutting off*) (Lev. 22:9). In the case of karet, the kohen is *cut off* from future altar service. In other words, where a breach of holiness occurs, one strike and you’re out!

? *Read Lev. 21:23 and review Ex. 29:43. Joosten [p. 123] comments, “The holy presence of the godhead sanctifies the temple, which is therefore called the sanctuary (mikdash).” How can holiness radiate holiness to the sanctuary?*

Gifts for God

"ADONAI said to Moshe, "Speak to Aharon . . . 'When anyone . . . brings his offering . . . to ADONAI as a burnt offering . . . to be accepted, you must bring a male without defect . . ."" —Lev. 22:17-19

Voluntary offerings can be neder (*a vow, votive offering*) or n'davah (*a free will, voluntary offering*). The neder must be tam (*whole, perfect*), without blemish. The n'davah need not be tam (Lev. 22:23), since it could be sold (not put on the altar) and the proceeds donated to the sanctuary.

As voluntary offerings, these sacrifices can be wholly given to God as an olah (*ascent*) or shared as sh'lamim (*fellowship offerings*) among worshippers, kohanim, and God.

Vows are serious matters that must be wholly fulfilled. One's word must be kept, and kept perfectly. Any blemish, any imperfection or shortfall, renders the vow unacceptable.

Vows must be kept perfectly.

Upon completion of a vow, the offerer's neder must be an unblemished, male sacrifice from the cattle, sheep, or goats. The adage, "Half a loaf is better than no loaf at all" does not apply to vows. Better never to vow than to try one's best and fall short! (Lev. 22:20)

? Compare the descriptions that render both sacrifices and kohanim unfit for the altar (Lev. 21:18-20, 22:22-24). List five blemishes common to both kohanim and sacrifices. Explain how priests must be acceptable as living sacrifices.

Proclaiming Holy Times

“ ***Adonai said to Moshe, “Tell the people of Isra’el: ‘The designated times of Adonai which you are to proclaim as holy convocations are my designated times.’” ”***

—Leviticus 23:1-2

Declare the times as holy and then they become holy—even if said unwittingly or in error [Sifra]. “You are to proclaim as holy . . . my designated times” (Lev. 23:2).

Proclaim holiness at the appointed times.

Torah attributes holiness to persons, places, objects, and special times [Levine, p. 257]. L’kiddesh otoh (*to sanctify it, to declare it holy*) is accomplished through ritual, prayer, and formal declaration.

Shabbat is the first mo’ed (*appointed time*). Torah calls the Shabbat day a mikra’ei kodesh (*proclamation of holiness*), which prohibits m’lach’ah (*assigned tasks, work*) (Lev. 23:2-3). On this day, Shabbat is declared holy, set apart for God.

In temple times, witnesses would report (cf. Lev. 23:1), and then the court would declare the day holy. Even if witnesses acted deceitfully or if the court sanctified the day without witnesses, the declaration would stand—but not if darkness fell before the court could formalize the declaration!

? ***Read Lev. 23:11, 16. Explain why the new barley/wheat is offered mi-mochorat ha-shabbat (on the morrow of the Shabbat). Is the seventh day of Pesach (Lev. 23:8) also the seventh day of counting the omer? Explain why not.***

Time to Repent

"* ADONAI *said to Moshe, "Tell the people of Isra'el, 'In the seventh month, the first of the month is to be . . . a holy convocation announced with blasts on the shofar.'" "

—Leviticus 23:23-24

Sabbaticals predominate the Hebrew calendar. Torah marks the seventh month as zichron t'ru'ah (*a reminder by horn-blasting*) (Fox, Lev. 23:24, note p. 621). The "sh'varim-t'ru'ah" mimics the distressed sigh of a man coming before God's throne on the day of judgment [R.H. 34a].

Repentance precedes times of rest and rejoicing.

Called Rosh haShanah (*the Head of the Year*), this actual name never appears in Torah. Talmud calls Rosh haShanah the anniversary of the creation of Adam. "On Rosh haShanah all that comes into the world pass before Him like flocks of sheep" [Mishnah, R.H. 1.2].

Nine days after Yom T'ru-ah (*the day of horn-blasting*) is Yom haKippurim (*the day of atonements*) (Lev. 23:24, 27). Now called Yom Kippur, the plural (or superlative) use by Torah marks the day when God is favorably predisposed to show the greatest mercy! Thus, Yom T'ruah becomes the day of justice with mercy, and Yom Kippur becomes the day of mercy with justice [Ramban].

? Read Lev. 23:27-30. Why does God require every soul in the nation to afflict itself on the greatest day of mercy? Read 1 Thess. 4:16-17. Explain why the rapture could be fulfilled on Yom T'ruah. Relate this to being "born again."

Time to Rejoice 

> *“Adonai said to Moshe, “Tell the people of Isra'el, ‘On the fifteenth day of this seventh month is the feast of Sukkot for seven days to Adonai.’” ”*
>
> *—Leviticus 23:33-34*

Proclaim holiness! Cease from all m'lechet avodah (*servile work*), starting on the full moon, the day that the power of the seventh month peaks. Thus, the time commences for redemption of paradise on earth!

> ***Sukkot and Sh'mini Atseret mark times of rejoicing in redemption.***

Sukkot (*huts, booths*) celebrates the final harvest festival. The Promised Land ripens with grapes, olives, dates, figs, pomegranates, wheat, and barley. Harvesting these firstfruits anticipates transforming the Land of Promise into a mini-paradise on earth (Lev. 23:39). Joy of the harvest and the ceasing of servile labor project the hope of re-entering Gan Eden (*the Garden of Eden/Paradise*). Offering firstfruits and firstborn cattle redeems not only nations, but even creation itself!

Sukkot lasts a week, which gives Yisra'el a Shabbat rest in the Land, amidst fruitfulness and joyous celebration. Then commences the last holy day of Torah, Sh'mini Atseret (*eighth termination*) (Lev. 23:36), the day in which the Torah is fulfilled!

? ***Read Num. 29:12-34, 35-38. Yisra'el sacrifices 70 bulls, one for each nation; then on Sh'mini Atseret, Yisra'el tarries an extra, 8th day, and sacrifices for itself a lone bull. Describe Yisra'el's priestly intercession among the nations.***

Feasting on Holiness

❝ *ADONAI said to Moshe, "Order the people of Isra'el to bring you pure oil from crushed olives for the light, to keep lamps burning always."* ❞

—Leviticus 24:1-2

Priests eat holy loaves in the Lord's Presence in a holy place (Lev. 24:9). The kohanim must nurture a desire for holiness, a desire beyond eating good food in a godly place. Man is created to fellowship with His Creator and enjoy Him forever!

Taste and see that holiness is delightful!

God commands Yisra'el to supply pure oil which gives a pure light to the tabernacle. His command extends across the generations and sets apart Yisra'el as a pure and holy light to the nations!

The lightly pressed olives are crushed merely by their own weight, as brimming baskets are stacked high. Impurities would darken this oil and cause the light to flicker, but pure oil casts a pure light in the holy place.

The kohanim arrange lampwicks, bread, and even frankincense to be burned as a fire offering unto the LORD (Lev. 24:2, 7). In this holy place, the ritually pure eat the holy loaves, called kodesh kodashim (*especially holy*) (Lev. 23:4-8), under the watchful gaze of the LORD.

? ***Read 1 Sam. 21:2-6(3-7תנ"ך), cf. Mt. 12:1-8. Did David eat kodesh kodashim in a holy place? Verify whether or not David and his men were ritually pure when they ate the bread. How could the kohen give David consecrated bread?***

Keeping the Camp Pure

> *" So Moshe spoke to the people of Isra'el, and they took the man who had cursed outside the camp and stoned him to death. Thus the people of Isra'el did as ADONAI had ordered Moshe. " —Leviticus 24:23*

Moshe consults God in the first matter to be clarified by God Himself (Lev. 24:10-12). God decrees death to the ger (*sojourner*) who blasphemed His name (Lev. 24:13-14).

Keep the holy within and the unholy without.

According to Torah, anyone who curses God shall bear his sin (Lev. 24:15-16). Rules for stoning require s'michah (*laying on of hands*), a ceremony in which witnesses identify the executed as bearing his own sin. The entire community responds to the divine decree by casting stones in immediate obedience, ka'asher tsivah ADONAI et Moshe (*exactly as the LORD commanded Moshe*) (Lev. 24:23).

Punishing the ger establishes the fact that there is one law for the citizen and the resident alien alike (Lev. 24:22). Carrying out the punishment keeps the camp pure. Punishment not only removes the accursed one from the camp (Lev. 24:14, 23), but it also brings together the entire community to sanctify God's name.

***?** Read Jn. 8:2-7, cf. Lev. 24:14. Torah-teachers confront Yeshua and ask for a ruling on stoning a woman caught in the act of adultery. Did Yeshua's response address the witnesses as conspirators or adulterers? Defend your answer.*

Holy Living — *Meander*

> *“The cohanim are not to eat anything, bird or animal, that dies naturally or is torn to death.”*
>
> —*Ezekiel 44:31*

The most holy must stay most holy by living most holy lives. Kohanim teach the people to separate the kodesh (*holy*) from the chol (*common*) and the tamei (*impure*) from the tahor (*pure*).

Kohanim live pure and holy lives before the LORD.

The kohanim must set the example that they impart to others. Priests are to reserve the fat and blood from all sacrifices for the LORD alone (Ez. 44:15). They must wear consecrated linens when in the holy place (Ez. 44:18). In fact, they must keep the linens in the holy place, lest the garments touch the people and consecrate them with holiness (Ez. 44:19). Nor can kohanim drink wine when on duty (Ez. 44:21).

They must marry consecrated women, whether virgins or widows of priests (Ez. 44:22). Kohanim who eat in the holy Presence of God must eat foods that are not only kosher, but also untouched by impure hands (Ez. 44:29-31). In short, the priests live lives completely saturated by holiness.

? *Read Ez. 44:30. Explain how giving holy gifts to the priests culminates in blessings bestowed on the house of the one who gives. How is holiness spread to the nation? How is Yisra'el sanctified by sanctifying her kohanim?*

...ings Feasting at God's Banquet

"I tell you, not one of those who were invited will get a taste of my banquet!"

—Luke 14:24

The parable of the great supper describes a grand banquet in the making. Formal invitations are sent and implicitly accepted.

All who respond can eat at God's house.

Afterward, extensive preparations are completed. The host sends his servant to inform the invitees, who then respond with refusals that needed to have been communicated before preparations began (Lk. 14:16-20). Understandably, these tardy excuses enrage the host, who suddenly faces the embarrassment of vacant seats. He invites new guests: the poor, crippled, lame, and blind (Lk. 14:13, 21). Empty spaces remain, so invitations are extended a third time!

Now the servant goes to the highways outside where the ger (*resident alien*) travels, and to the hedges where beggars search for food left in the corners of the vineyard (Lk. 14:23). The servant urges even strangers to attend, for the host insists on a full house for supper. Most certainly, the house *will* be filled!

? *Review Lk. 14:13-14, 21, 23-24. Talmud says that priests who are poor, crippled, lame, or blind can eat kodashim, as can the ger of a priestly household. Explain the implications for believer-priests invited to feast at Yeshua's house.*

Talk Your Walk . . .

EMOR (*say!*) to the kohanim, 'Be holy!' and lead the people, by example, to draw near to God. Priests are subject to higher standards, because they live in close proximity to the manifest Presence of the living God.

Priests' lives must be wholesome. The kohanim must be properly clothed and ritually pure in order to minister before the LORD. They represent the nation when they kindle the light and start the day with the daily offering, a heartfelt gift for God. The priest who offers an unblemished sacrifice must himself be a living, unblemished sacrifice. Priestly fellowship with God sets the standards for the nation. A holy priesthood leads a nation to live as a mamlechet kohanim v'goy kadosh (*kingdom of priests and a holy nation*). In this way, the priests call all Yisra'el to a holy lifestyle.

Priests set the tone for a holy nation.

Keeping one's word characterizes a holy camp. Eating in a state of ritual purity characterizes the call to fellowship in the Presence of the living God. Proclaiming holy times through ritual, prayer, and formal declaration sanctifies the seasons. It sets a pattern for repentance and purity to be followed by seasons of rejoicing and fruitfulness in the camp and, eventually, in the Land God swore to give to the patriarchs and their ancestors. God is holy, and those who desire to live in His Presence must learn to live holy lives.

Oasis

. . . Walk Your Talk

The psalmist proclaims, "Taste and see that the LORD is good" (Ps. 34:8(9תנ״ך)). Cultivating a taste for holiness could be the greatest calling given to man! Those who are holy draw near to God. "The effectual fervent prayer of a righteous man availeth much" (James 5:16b, KJV). Do you draw near to God? Would your ministry be more effective if your fervency burned hot for God? Is holiness the fire that fuels your prayer? Is holiness your heart's desire?

We must take seriously the truth that believers in covenant with Yeshua have tasted that the LORD is good (1 Pet. 2:3). God Himself is building up believers as kohanim set apart to offer spiritual sacrifices that are acceptable to God (1 Pet. 2:5). Messiah has modeled priestly behavior, and He calls all believers to follow His priestly example! Remember that firstborns were once the priests of their households, before the Levites inherited the priesthood on behalf of the nation. Now, believers follow Messiah in faith to become firstborns from the dead. The journey begins spiritually when you present yourself as a holy and living sacrifice. The priestly calling starts there! How are *you* called to sacrifice?

> ***You are called to be a living sacrifice.***

Shabbat Shalom!

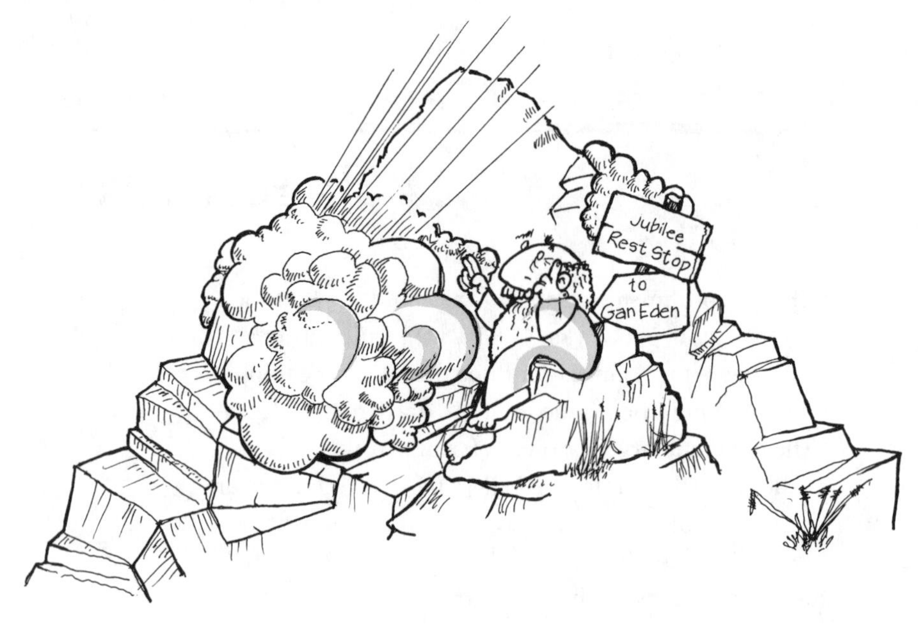

בהר, on Mount Sinai,
the LORD God did talk
to Moshe
about how the people should walk.
"Count years up to seven,
then plant not a stalk.
For the land needs to rest.
Have faith and don't balk!

"You're resident aliens
living with Me.
The land is all Mine!
And on Jubilee,
whatever was sold gets redeemed.
Whoopee!
Hebrew slaves go free
and proclaim liberty!"

Walk B'Har!
25:1-26:2

On the Mount

Torah—Leviticus 25:1-26:2

1st Sabbatical on the Mount—Leviticus 25:1-2
2nd Jubilee—Leviticus 25:14-15
3rd Dwelling Securely—Leviticus 25:19
4th Redeeming the Land—Leviticus 25:25
5th Redeeming Households—Leviticus 25:29
6th Redeeming the Unhoused—Leviticus 25:39-40
7th Redeeming All Yisra'el—Leviticus 25:47-48
Maftir Dwelling with God—Leviticus 26:2

Haftarah—Jeremiah 32:6-27

Kinsman Redeemer—Jeremiah 32:27

B'rit Chadashah—Luke 4:16-21

Liberty Proclaimed!—Luke 4:21

On Mount Sinai,
Holiness Rules

Looking Back

VAYIKRA ADONAI (*and the Lord called*) Moshe to come near to the Tent of Meeting, saying: TSAV (*command!*) the kohanim to keep the camp pure. Kohanim must be cleansed, clothed, and elevated to a ritually pure and holy life. The LORD and His holiness must be the desire of the priest!

Consecrated for seven days, the priests enter the holy sphere with care and represent the nation ba-yom ha-SH'MINI (*on the eighth day*). But Nadav and Avihu err, kindling the wrath of God.

The impure and the holy cannot co-exist in the same space. A woman who TAZRIA (*bears seed*) must wait to approach the altar. The M'TSORA (*infected one*) is barred!

VAYIKRA—*and He called Moshe and the nation to draw near, saying,* TSAV *the kohanim to keep the camp holy. Raise them up on day* SH'MINI.

The woman who* TAZRIA *must wait to re-enter the camp. The* M'TSORA *is barred.* ACHAREI MOT *of his sons, even Aharon must approach with care.

We all are called to keep the commands and be* K'DOSHIM. *The Lord tells Moshe,* EMOR, *say to the priests, maintain high standards for a holy God* B'HAR—*on the Mount!

ACHAREI MOT (*after the death*), the holy place needs cleansing from the pollution of Aharon's fallen sons. God limits entry into the Holy of Holies to once each year, and that time only to cleanse the nation of sins that pile up on

Log

the altar and threaten to drive God from the camp.

K'DOSHIM (*holy ones*), you are to become like the Holy One of Yisra'el in all your actions. Live in covenant with God as a kingdom of priests and a holy nation.

God further instructs Moshe: **EMOR** (*say!*) to the priests that holy standards increase for those who live in closest proximity to God. Perfect holiness means fitting into God's picture and using ritual procedures to maintain purity. Holy times must be proclaimed, and the entire camp must be purified yearly.

The drive toward holiness, so natural **B'HAR** Sinai (*on Mt. Sinai*), must continue to characterize the ways of daily life. Holiness must be grounded in the institutions and in the people who live in the communal sphere of the Holy One Himself. Only a holy nation can abide in proximity to a holy God . . .

In B'HAR . . .

The Key Person is Moshe (*Moses*).

The Scene is the tabernacle, in the wilderness of Sinai.

Main Events include instructions upon entering the Land, to take Shabbat, leave fields fallow the seventh year, and observe Jubilee the fiftieth year by returning all property to original owners; special guidelines for a relative or the poor person himself to redeem what was sold; houses in walled cities redeemable only the first year; houses redeemable by Levites at any time; no usury; no harsh treatment for hired servants; Israelites selling themselves to strangers redeemable or set free at Jubilee; children of Yisra'el as God's own servants; no idols; and commands to keep Shabbat and revere the sanctuary.

The Trail Ahead

The Path

	ר	הַ	בְּ
letter:	reish	hay	bet
sound:	R	**Ha**	B’

on Mount = B’HAR = **בהר**

Work

The Legend

and spoke the LORD	*va-y'da**ber** ADONAI*	וַיְדַבֵּר יְהוָה
to Moses	*el-Mo**she***	אֶל־מֹשֶׁה
on Mt. Sinai,	*b'**Har** Si**nai***	בְּהַר סִינַי
saying, speak	*le**mor** da**ber***	לֵאמֹר׃ דַּבֵּר
to the sons of Israel	*el-b'**nei** Yisra'**el***	אֶל־בְּנֵי יִשְׂרָאֵל
& you shall say to them	*v'amar**ta** ale**hem***	וְאָמַרְתָּ אֲלֵהֶם
that you will enter	*ki ta**vo**'oo*	כִּי תָבֹאוּ
into the land that	*el ha-**a**rets **a**sher*	אֶל־הָאָרֶץ אֲשֶׁר
I am giving to you-all,	*A**ni** no**ten** la**chem***	אֲנִי נֹתֵן לָכֶם
& will 'Sabbath' the land	*v'shav'**tah** ha-**a**rets*	וְשָׁבְתָה הָאָרֶץ
a Sabbath to the LORD	*shab**bat** la-ADONAI*	שַׁבָּת לַיהוָה׃

—*Leviticus 25:1-2*

Related Words

mountain	*har*	הַר
Mt. Sinai	*Har Si**nai***	הַר סִינַי
Mt. Zion	*Har Tsi**on***	הַר צִיּוֹן
Mt. of Olives	*Har Zei**tim***	הַר זֵיתִים
volcano (mt. of fire)	*har esh*	הַר אֵשׁ
mighty men (mountains of the world)	*ha**rei** o**lam***	הָרֵי עוֹלָם
how beautiful upon the mountains (Is. 52:7)	*mah na**vu** al-he-ha**rim***	מַה־נָּאווּ עַל־הֶהָרִים

Hit the Trail!

Sabbatical on the Mount

> ❝ *ADONAI spoke to Moshe on Mount Sinai; he said, "Tell the people of Isra'el, 'When you enter the land I am giving you, the land itself is to observe a Shabbat rest for ADONAI.'"* ❞ *—Leviticus 25:1-2*

Sh'mittah (*release* on sabbatical year) is compared to Shabbat among the festivals of Torah. Sh'mittah celebrates God's ownership over the Land, and it mandates shavtah la'aretz (*Sabbath-ceasing for the Land*).

> ***Let the Land rest every seventh year.***

Ceasing requires prohibitions on sowing, pruning, reaping, gathering, and selling produce for profit, every seventh year (Lev. 25:2-7, Ex. 23:10-11, Dt. 15:1-3). Sh'mittah applies the concept of the Nazirite vow to the Land: the "aftergrowth" of harvest is left growing like the unkempt hair of a Nazirite (Num. 6:5); the grapes of nazir (*consecrated*) vines are not gathered; and, Sabbath-ceasing means no m'lachah (*assigned tasks*)! Sh'mittah affirms that God owns the Land.

Debtors go free in the Sh'mittah year. Households celebrate equality: servants, hired hands, resident aliens, foreigners, flocks, and even wild beasts share together in eating the produce that comes up on its own (Lev. 25:6-7).

? *Read Lev. 25:10-13. Compare/contrast Sh'mittah with Yovel (Homebringing). Avot 5:9 says that failure to observe Sh'mittah or Yovel causes exile. How can disrespect for God's ownership of the Land cause exile for Yisra'el?*

Jubilee

“ If you sell anything to your neighbor or buy anything from him, neither of you is to exploit the other. Rather, you are to take into account the number of years after the yovel . . . ”—Lev. 25:14-15

Sanctify the fiftieth year! Proclaim d'ror (*liberty*!) for all inhabitants (Lev. 25:10), every man to his clan and every clan to its land! All Hebrew slaves go free, even those with pierced ears who refuse their freedom!

Proclaim liberty for all!

This segment cautions against trying to sell land in perpetuity (Lev. 25:14, 17). The LORD owns all the Land! Labor and crop yields can be sold, but not land. Since fields revert to the ancestral owners every fifty years, the selling price of Land diminishes each year. The year before Jubilee, the price of Land is not even one year's harvest (Lev. 25:16).

Yovel (*Jubilee, Homebringing*) creates a constructive tension between capitalism (which rewards owners of capital and land) and communism (which accords equal status to all). Yovel eliminates oppression across generations. Every fifty years, clans receive back their original territories, including all improvements to their holdings.

? Read Lev. 25:9. Explain why the shofar sounds, inaugurating the Yovel, on Yom Kippur. Why is the tenth day of the seventh month the perfect occasion for starting the Yovel? Why should purity precede liberty and rejoicing?

Dwelling Securely

> *❝ The land will yield its produce, you will eat until you have enough, and you will live there securely. ❞*
>
> *—Leviticus 25:19*

Security comes from living in God's Presence on God's Land. Yisra'el must never forget her status as gerim v'toshavim (*sojourners and resident-settlers*), set free by God and granted asylum on sanctuary land (Lev. 25:23).

Those who keep Sh'mittah will prosper in the Land.

God's covenant stipulates that Yisra'el will prosper and dwell securely in the Land. The nation must obey Torah, including the chukim (*statutes* governing agriculture) and mishpatim (*ordinances* governing the release of slaves and ancestral lands) [Ramban, Lev. 25:18]. Sh'mittah (*release* on sabbatical year) guarantees God's miraculous provision of a triple harvest from the sixth year's plantings (Lev. 25:21). Such a guarantee flies in the face of human logic!

For this reason, Torah classifies agricultural requirements as chukim (*statutes*), not as mitzvot (*commands*) or mishpatim (*ordinances*) which are based on rationality or logic. Clearly, dwelling securely in the Land demands radical faith!

? How does God's ownership of the Land (Lev. 25:23; Ex. 15:17; Is. 14:2, 25; Jer. 2:7; Ez. 36:5, 38:16; Hos. 9:3; Ps. 10:15(16תנ"ך), 85:1(2תנ"ך)) transform your understanding of the parable of the wicked vinedressers (Mt. 21:33-46)?

Redeeming the Land

" That is, if one of you becomes poor and sells some of his property, his next-of-kin can come and buy back what his relative sold. "

—Leviticus 25:25

Failure to observe the covenant sets Yisra'el on a spiritual path that leads back to slavery in Egypt.

Torah requires next-of-kin to redeem ancestral lands.

The descent spirals from loss of moveable property (Lev. 25:14) to the forced sale of ancestral lands (Lev. 25:25-28), loss of one's house (vv. 29-31), debt (v. 36), servanthood (v. 39), and selling oneself to a non-Jew whose family serves idols [v. 47, Rashi].

An Israelite must be impoverished before Torah permits him to sell ancestral lands. The principle that God owns all Land immediately obligates relatives of the impoverished to redeem the sold property.

Kinsman redeemers can purchase back property even against the will of the buyer, after a two-year waiting period [Rashi; Kidd. 21]. But if no one pays the price of redemption, then at Yovel (*Homebringing*), the shofar proclaims, "Every man to his clan, and every clan to its Land!"

? *Read Roman 11:25-27. Notice that God sent Messiah only after Yisra'el had descended into spiritual bondage to an idolatrous empire. What does Messiah do, as kinsman redeemer, when he comes to take away Yisra'el's sins?*

Redeeming Households

"If someone sells a dwelling in a walled city, he has one year after the date of sale in which to redeem it. For a full year he will have the right of redemption . . . " ***—Leviticus 25:29***

Three kinds of houses are described in this segment: the beit moshav (*residential house*) in a walled city; the beit ha-chatser (*village house*) in an unwalled city; and the house of a Levite.

God calls kinsmen to redeem households from the cycle of poverty.

The beit moshav refers to commercial areas and artisan shops residing in fortified cities (Lev. 25:24-30). If these houses are sold, kinsmen have up to a year to redeem them; or they are lost in perpetuity.

The beit ha-chatser describes a village house located on farm land, surrounded by open spaces (Lev. 25:31). Kinsmen must redeem these houses, or else the impoverished must wait for Yovel (*Homebringing*). Farms consecrated to the sanctuary must be redeemed or pass to the kohanim (Lev. 27:20-21).

Thus, only houses in Levitical cities possess a heritage that can never be lost. The g'ulat olam (*redemption right for the ages*) assures permanent housing for those who are consecrated to the LORD.

? Torah depicts ger toshavim (resident-settlers) as gentiles who settle on sanctuary lands and refrain from idolatry, but still eat unkosher food [Rashi]. Read Lev. 25:35, Acts 15:19-20. Are New Covenant priests ger toshavim? Explain.

Redeeming the Unhoused

"If a member of your people has become poor among you and sells himself to you, do not make him do the work of a slave. Rather . . . treat him like an employee or a tenant . . . " ***—Lev. 25:39-40***

Those who lose houses and incur debts must not lose status as citizens in God's household. Rather, Torah requires that an indentured Israelite be treated as an employee, a hired hand or a ger toshav (*resident-settler*) [Fox, p. 633].

Do not degrade those who lose their houses.

Torah discourages oppression (Lev. 25:38). Talmud adds, "One who buys himself a slave buys himself a master" [Kidd. 75a]. Degrading tasks must not be assigned, but rather natural capacities must be employed, whether skilled work fitting a hired hand or field labor fitting a toshav (*settler*). In any event, at Yovel (*Homebringing*), the Jewish servant must go free, along with his household (Lev. 25:40-41).

One might ask why, then, does the alien slave not have similar rights (Lev. 25:44-46). Here, the analog reflects donation of houses to the sanctuary. As the kohanim have holy status within Yisra'el, so now Yisra'el has collective status as holy among the nations!

? Study Acts 2:42-47. Explain how the New Covenant believers first treated those in their midst who were indebted or homeless. Explain how the Ruach rewarded kinsmen redeemers for setting free the impoverished brethren.

Redeeming All Yisra'el

" If a foreigner living among you has grown rich, and a member of your people has become poor and sells himself to this foreigner . . . he may be redeemed after he has been sold . . . " —Lev. 25:47-48

The case in which an impoverished Israelite sells himself to a ger (*resident alien*) or to an eker (*offshoot*) of the ger's clan is the grimmest circumstance of all (Lev. 25:47).

Torah prohibits enslaving its citizens forever.

Despite this degradation, one's right to mercy is not forfeited! Kinsmen must redeem or await Yovel (*Jubilee, Homebringing*), as in all other cases (Lev. 25:25-28, 35-38, 39-43, 47-55). Thus, the prosperous ger living in community must obey a rule that disadvantages himself. Because he lives near God's dwelling, the unconverted ger must observe all prohibitions (Lev. 25:53; 26:1), out of fear of defiling the Land and sanctuary of God. Neither idolatry, nor perpetual ownership of Land or God's chosen, is tolerated in God's House.

Torah mandates that every Israelite in God's house regain liberty and property. In fact, at Yovel, even the Israelite slave, who pierces his ear and chooses bondage, must go free!

? *Review Lev. 25:44-46. Hebrew servants must go free at Jubilee, but the gerim can be enslaved for life. Is this a double standard? What is the sense of mandating prohibitions for the ger, but not performative (positive) commands?*

Dwelling with God

" Keep my Shabbats, and revere my sanctuary; I am ADONAI. "

—Leviticus 26:2

Dwelling with God requires the nation, both Yisra'el and ger, to adopt a holy lifestyle, for "I, ADONAI your God, am holy" (Lev. 19:2; cf. Lev. 18:30c, 19:3c, 19:4c, 25:55c, 26:1c, 2c).

A holy God calls a holy people to radiate holiness.

Holiness must touch every area of life. This maftir functions as a grand conclusion for the second half of the book. Yisra'el must, above all, resist idolatry and the path of descent leading to Egypt (Lev. 25:55, cf. v. 47). In addition, she must keep Shabbats and remain on the holy path of ascent, including observing Sh'mittah and Yovel (Lev. 26:1) and approaching with reverence God's holy dwelling (Lev. 26:2).

In the broadest sense, God's call for Moshe and the nation to draw near to Him as a mamlechet kohanim and goy kadosh (*kingdom of priests* and *a holy nation*) reaches its summit. B'HAR Sinai (*on Mount Sinai*), God separates the nation to be holy to Him and to radiate holiness to the nations!

? Review the maftir. Ramban says that the maftir summarizes the holy times of the nation. Relate the avoidance of idolatry to Pesach, keeping Shabbats to Shavu'ot, and holding-in-awe God's dwelling to Sukkot and Sh'mini Atseret.

Kinsman Redeemer *Meander*

“ Look, I am Adonai, the God of every living creature; is there anything too hard for me? ”

—Jeremiah 32:27

While imprisoned and during the siege of Y'rushalayim, Yirm'yahu (*Jeremiah*) hears the word of God—to redeem the property of his indebted kinsman, Chanam'el (*Favor of God*). Yet exile is prophesied for the next seventy years! (2 Chr. 36:21)

Yisra'el fails to keep Sh'mittah and reaps captivity.

The Land must rest under God's ownership, since the 70 Sh'mittot (sabbatical years/ *release*) have yet to be kept. Only then will God show mercy and return His captive people to the Land (Jer. 29:10).

Accordingly, God instructs Yirm'yahu to pay silver and write a deed of purchase to redeem the ancestral plot. Yirm'yahu deposits the legal document of redemption into long-term storage as a sign that the sons of Yisra'el will again return to buy and sell in the Land.

God leaves His people with an unfailing hope. His mercy never fails—even when exile and enslavement engulf His people, in a land where gentiles worship idols.

? Review Lev. 25:25, cf. Lev. 25:47-48, 54-55. Explain God's mercy to redeem the Land as a sign that loss of the Temple and the nation's exile is temporary. Can the millennium be based on 1000 Sh'mittah years owed to God? Explain.

...ings  Liberty Proclaimed!

"** He started to speak to them: "Today, as you heard it read, this passage of the Tanakh was fulfilled!" **"

—Luke 4:21

It is one thing to proclaim liberty (Lev. 25:10). Any prophet can proclaim liberty. It is quite another thing to authorize release. Only the Deliverer can set free the captives. This is a role reserved exclusively for the Messiah.

Messiah proclaims Yovel as the year of release.

Yeshua preached good news for the poor, release for the captives, sight for the blind, and liberty for the oppressed (Lk. 4:18, quoting Is. 61:1). He also proclaimed Yovel (*Homebringing*), "a year of the favor of ADONAI" (Lk. 4:19a, Is. 61:2a). Then, closing the haftarah scroll and with all eyes fixed on him, Yeshua told those at the Natzeret synagogue, "Today, as you heard it read, this passage of the Tanakh was fulfilled!" (Lk. 4:21).

But the Deliverer did not please the crowd by granting sight to the many. When he refused, the people of his home town tried to lynch him by hurling him from "the brow of the mountain" [Bock, p. 419 on Lk. 4:29].

? *Read Romans 11:25-27. The Redeemer/Deliverer refers to one who can liberate the nation from foreign oppression. Study Is. 61:2b. Explain why Yeshua halted his reading in mid-verse. Why would this anger the people of Natzeret?*

Talk Your Walk . . .

Moshe spends forty days completely alone with the LORD B'HAR (*on the Mount*). There, God speaks! Moshe receives instructions designed to guide the children of Yisra'el to ascend in holiness and rest with God in the high places.

God owns the Land. Sh'mittah (*release* on sabbatical year) requires that the Land rest every seventh year from sowing, pruning, gathering, harvesting, and commerce. During the Sh'mittah, men, women, children, hired hands, servants, sojourners, foreigners, domesticated animals, and even wild beasts have rights to the produce.

On the Mount, God calls man to rest with Him.

Yovel (*Jubilee, Homebringing*) follows immediately after the seventh Sh'mittah year. At Yom Kippur, the shofar proclaims liberation, all slaves go free, and all Land reverts to its original owners. The Jubilee assures new beginnings for families, clans, and the impoverished. Such legislation promises fruitfulness and security from famine, plagues, and enemies.

In addition, since God has acquired His people by bringing them out of Egypt, no one else can own them in perpetuity. Thus, God and His people rest together and make the Land a fruitful paradise. In this context, Sh'mittah and the Yovel point to restoring Gan Eden and man's call to rest with God!

Oasis

. . . Walk Your Talk

Romans 6:22 says, "However, now, freed from sin and enslaved to God, you do get the benefit—it consists in being made holy, set apart for God, and its end result is eternal life." Messianic believers celebrate their redemption from Egypt and their redemption from sin and death by being enslaved to God. In both instances, redemption means servanthood to God.

Moshe walked the path of holiness from the sacred ground near the burning bush to the cloud-enshrouded summit of Mount Sinai. There, God called Moshe to spend forty days without food or drink, in the glory of His presence. Moshe's entire life prepared him for this moment.

God also calls *you* out of this world, to ascend into His Presence. Your entire life prepares you for that moment. Study your life. How can you integrate sabbatical rest into your lifestyle? How can you prepare to rule with Him at the millennium? "Blessed and holy is anyone who has a part in the first resurrection" (Rev. 20:6). Will you be there?

Prepare to enter the holy Presence of God.

בחקתי—in My statutes,
be strong.
Stay holy to Me,
that means all day long!
If you harden your hearts
and do what is wrong,
you'll lose all the land
and be sad, with no song.

So mend your hearts,
walk closely with Me.
Obey My statutes,
live merrily.
Let your heart praise God.
Say, "Great is He!"
With your head held high,
walk holy and free!

Walk B'CHUKOTAI!
26:3-27:34

In My statutes

TORAH—Leviticus 26:3-27:34

1st Walk—Leviticus 26:3-4
2nd Security—Leviticus 26:6
3rd Surplus—Leviticus 26:10
4th Value—Leviticus 27:1-3
5th Ancestral Fields—Leviticus 27:16
6th Purchased Fields—Leviticus 27:22-23
7th Not Redeemable—Leviticus 27:29
Maftir Concluding Statement—Leviticus 27:34

HAFTARAH—Jeremiah 16:19-17:14

Witness to the Nations—Jeremiah 17:14

B'RIT CHADASHAH—Matthew 22:1-14

Election—Matthew 22:14

In My Statutes
Is the Path of Blessing

Looking Back

VAYIKRA ADONAI (*and the LORD called*) Moshe to come near to the Tent of Meeting, saying: TSAV (*command!*) the kohanim to keep the camp pure. Consecration elevates the priests to lead a ritually pure and holy life in close proximity to God.

VAYIKRA, *and He called Moshe and the nation, to draw near, saying,* TSAV *the priests to keep the camp holy. Raise them up on day* SH'MINI.

The woman who* TAZRIA *must wait to re-enter camp. The* M'TSORA *must be barred.* ACHAREI MOT, *even the High Priest approaches God with care.

***We all are called to be* K'DOSHIM. *But* EMOR *to the priests, maintain even higher standards for a holy God* B'HAR.**

B'CHUKOTAI, *in My statutes, are blessings for the nation in covenant with God!*

Then ba-yom ha-SH'MINI (*on the eighth day*), the kohanim begin their service. But Nadav and Avihu die, contaminating the holy place. Their unauthorized entry kindles the wrath of God. In like manner, a woman who TAZRIA (*bears seed*) must wait after childbirth before she approaches the altar. Unless healed by God, the M'TSORA (*infected one*) remains barred forever!

ACHAREI MOT (*after the death*), the holy place needs cleansing from pollution. God limits entry into the Holy of Holies. Only on Yom Kippur may the Kohen Gadol (*High Priest*), properly clothed and anointed, enter to cleanse the nation of sins piled up on the altar and threatening to drive God from the camp. God tells Moshe to say: K'DOSHIM (*holy ones*), become like the Holy One of Yisra'el in all your actions. You are born in the Land, commanded not to eat forbidden fruits, and called to covenant as a kingdom of priests and a holy nation.

Furthermore, **EMOR** (*say!*) to the priests that standards for holiness increase for those living in proximity to God. Perfect holiness means fitting into God's picture and observing ritual procedures to maintain the camp's purity. Holy days must be proclaimed at Torah- appointed times.

The struggle for holiness, so easily observed **B'HAR** (*on the Mount*), must characterize life in society. Yisra'el's institutions and people must be grounded on holiness. Only a holy nation can abide in proximity to a holy God.

In B'CHUKOTAI . . .

The Key People are Moshe (*Moses*) and the children of Yisra'el (*Israel*).

The Scene is the tabernacle, in the wilderness of Sinai.

Main Events include God's promises of blessing for those who walk in His statutes and judgment for those who do not obey Him; warnings of being scattered among the nations, but also of remembering the covenant if iniquity is confessed; valuations placed on people, animals, homes, and property to be consecrated to the LORD; "These are the commandments which the LORD commanded Moshe for the children of Yisra'el on Mt. Sinai" (27:34).

What a promise! God will reward covenant obedience "**B'CHUKOTAI** (*in My statutes*)" with fruitfulness, surpluses, long life in the Land, and walking in freedom with heads held high . . .

The Trail Ahead

The Path

	י	תַ	קֹ	חֻ	בְּ
letter:	yod	tav	koof	chet	bet
sound:	EE	**Tah**	Koh	CHoo	B’

in My statutes = B’CHUKOTAI = **בחקתי**

The Legend

if <u>in my statutes</u>	*im-<u>b'chuko**tai**</u>*	אִם־בְּחֻקֹּתַי
you will walk	*te**le**choo*	תֵּלֵכוּ
& — commandments-my	*v'et-mitsvo**tai***	וְאֶת־מִצְוֹתַי
you-all will keep	*tish'm'**roo***	תִּשְׁמְרוּ
and you-all will do them,	*va-asi**tem** o**tam***	וַעֲשִׂיתֶם אֹתָם׃
then I will give rains-your	*v'nata**ti** gishmei**chem***	וְנָתַתִּי גִשְׁמֵיכֶם
in season-their	*b'i**tam***	בְּעִתָּם
and will give the land	*v'nat'**nah** ha'**a**rets*	וְנָתְנָה הָאָרֶץ
produce-her	*y'voo**lah***	יְבוּלָהּ
and tree of the field	*v'**ets** ha'sa**deh***	וְעֵץ הַשָּׂדֶה
will give fruit-his	*yi**ten** pir'**yo***	יִתֵּן פִּרְיוֹ׃

—*Leviticus 26:3-4*

Related Words

statute, custom, law, decree	*chok*	חֹק
constitution, ordinance	*choo**kah***	חֻקָּה
everlasting statute	*chok o**lam***	חֹק עוֹלָם
law-abiding	*sho**mer** chok*	שׁוֹמֵר חֹק
without limit	*liv**li** chok*	לִבְלִי חֹק
legal/illegal	*choo**ki**/lo-choo**ki***	חֻקִּי/לֹא־חֻקִּי
international law	*chok bein-leu**mi***	חֹק בֵּין־לְאֻמִּי

Hit the Trail!

Walk

" If you live by my regulations, observe my mitzvot and obey them; then I will provide the rain . . . in its season, the land will yield its produce, and the trees in the field . . . their fruit. " —Lev. 26:3-4

Walking in covenant assures rain in its season. Only if Yisra'el walks B'CHUKOTAI (*in My statutes*) and keeps God's commandments (Lev. 26:3-4), can she be assured that she walks in obedience to God.

God rewards obedience to the covenant with fruitfulness in the land.

The Land of Promise has few rivers or lakes. Manna-fed in the wilderness, now Yisra'el continue their faith journey in a Land that must be rain-fed from heaven.

Obedience to the covenant assures Yisra'el prosperity and fruitfulness in the Land. The covenant relationship must not be confused with a contract. Yisra'el's relationship with her God is likened to a marriage, not a business deal.

In covenants, mercy overrides justice, and love overrides fairness. Walking in Torah is not impossible (Dt. 30:11-14). Dangers of legalism arise only when one keeps Torah to merit rain or to merit long life in the land. Yet a marriage can prosper even if one party is wrong most of the time!

? Read Romans 9:30-32. Explain how one can live Torah "by faith" or "by works" (Ro. 9:32). How can faith and law come together in a non-works oriented way? How can a law of righteousenss be characterized by faith?

Security

"I will give shalom in the land—you will lie down to sleep unafraid of anyone. I will rid the land of wild animals. The sword will not go through your land."
—Leviticus 26:6

In the verse above, God personally promises: natati SHALOM (*I will give peace*) . . . v'hiSHBATi chayah (*and I will cause-to-cease wild beasts*). God brings Shabbat Shalom to the Land. The blessings of Gan Eden begin to unfold.

The Land will begin to enjoy its Sabbaths!

The people will be secure from the bloodthirsty, whether animals or enemies! No army will venture to cross through the Land to wage war. In fact, "The sword will not go through your land" (Lev. 26:6). Security comes from a united people. Five will chase a hundred, and a hundred will chase a hundred times as many [Rashi].

God promises to prosper the nation in covenant with Him. Even now in the waterless wilderness of a dry and foreboding desert, the children of Yisra'el will never again thirst for security from the Nile, the greatest river on earth. Rather, rain falls from heaven! Yisra'el's walk in faith and obedience must continue B'CHUKOTAI (*in My statutes*).

? ***Study Lev. 26:3-4, 6, 9. The covenant is conditional upon obeying statutes and doing mitzvot. Rashi says obedience merits blessings. But does the covenant require merit? How can blessings flow apart from merit? Explain.***

Surplus

" You will eat all you want from last year's harvest and throw out what remains of the old to make room for the new. "

—Leviticus 26:10

Surpluses abound! Hithalachti b'toch'chem (*I will walk about in your midst*), va'olech et-chem kom'miyut (*and I shall cause you to walk upright*) (Lev. 26:12,13). God breaks the yoke of slavery, causing His people to walk with heads held high!!

Blessings abound in My statutes!

When Yisra'el fails to walk B'CHUKOTAI (*in My Statutes*), she loses her "upright" walk with God. Loss to enemies (Lev. 26:16-17) graduates to loss of fruitfulness (Lev. 26:18-20), which if treated b'keri (*with casualness* or *contempt*), likewise reaps keri from God (Lev. 26:21-22, 23-26, 27-30). First God sends wild animals, then barbaric peoples to siege the cities and tear down the high places. God stops accepting offerings from his people with uncircumcised hearts (Lev. 26:31, 41). Exile follows. Yisra'el rots, exiled in their enemies' lands. Even the survivors are devoured in enemy lands—until the Land is repaid its sabbaticals (Lev. 26:39, 43).

? ***Study Lev. 26:40. What three sins must Yisra'el confess? Explain God's response (Lev. 26:41, 43-44). Note that the people rot in exile before confession, but "enjoy/find-acceptance" in exile after confession (Lev. 26:39, 43). Explain.***

Value

❝ ADONAI said to Moshe, " . . . If someone makes a clearly defined vow to ADONAI to give him an amount equal to the value of a human being, the value . . . is to be fifty shekels . . . " ❞ —Lev. 27:1-3

Votive pledges of silver provide income for the sanctuary. Individuals can sell themselves to God. They can also sell their animals or their houses to God. Better to be in debt to God than to one's enemies!

Votive offerings support the sanctuary.

In most cases, the person or his clan will redeem the unfortunate or impoverished party who sells himself or his property. Thus, the amount pledged is taxed an additional fifth, in the case of property (Lev. 27:13,15).

Persons are valued according to their productive capacity, with males priced more than females and elders over sixty priced less than either productive males or females (Lev. 27:3-4, 7).

An infant, who attains the age of one month, is priced at the going rate of the pidyon ha-ben (*redemption of the* firstborn *son*) (Lev. 27:6; Num. 3:47; 18:15-16).

? *Review Lev. 27:1-8. Explain why redeeming persons who are pledged to the sanctuary does not require an additional assessment of one-fifth. Explain why verse 8 provides for a downward revision in value for the impoverished.*

Ancestral Fields

"If a person consecrates to Adonai part of a field belonging to his tribe's possession, you are to value it according to its production . . ."

—Leviticus 27:16

Loss of ancestral fields is a far more serious matter than loss of moveable property or temporary indebtedness. An achuzah (*holding*) strikes at the heart of the "land and seed" promises God vowed to Avraham, Yitzchak, and Ya'akov.

Land is valued according to its productive capacity.

True to principle, Torah bases valuations on the productive capacity of the Land, from Yovel to Yovel (*Homebringing to Homebringing*). The Jubilee assessment, valued by the kohen, is reduced year by year according to the time of the Yovel, when all holdings revert to their original owners (Lev. 27:18). The redemption price increases the assessment by one-fifth, providing silver for the sanctuary (Lev. 27:19).

Two circumstances result in loss of ancestral lands: the seller does not want to redeem the Land; or the seller who consecrates the Land has also already sold the land. Such Land becomes a holding of the kohanim and reverts to them at Yovel (Lev. 27:20-21).

? ***Review Lev. 25:10, 13, 14ff. Remember that Land cannot be sold, because it belongs to the Lord. Only its productive capacity, between Jubilees, can be transferred. How, then, can the sanctuary inherit unredeemed consecrations?***

Purchased Fields

> *" If he consecrates to ADONAI a field which he has bought . . . then the cohen is to calculate its value according to the years remaining until the year of yovel . . . "*
> *—Leviticus 27:22-23*

Purchase of fields by others is still subject to the laws of Yovel. These properties revert to the original owners, since only the crop yields can be purchased.

One can consecrate only what one owns.

Thus, the buyer of nonancestral fields can consecrate the crop yields purchased, but not the Land itself. Being another's achuzah (*holding*), the Land reverts to its original holder at Yovel (*Jubilee, Homebringing*) (Lev. 27:24).

Anything that is set aside as holy for the sanctuary or for the kohanim is called cherem (*set apart, restricted*). In war situations, objects designated as cherem were proscribed for common use and destroyed (cf. Josh. 6:17-18, etc.). Here, objects designated as cherem are reserved exclusively for needs of the sanctuary [Levine, p. 198].

Interestingly, firstborn sons, oxen, sheep, and goats already belong to the LORD. These cannot, then, be consecrated, because they belong to the LORD already (Lev. 27:26).

? *Read Lev. 27:22. What can the purchaser consecrate to God? Explain how firstlings from among the herds and flocks are sacred already (read Ex. 9:4-6; 13:2, 13-15). Now, relate consecration to God to the idea of ownership.*

Not Redeemable

"No person who has been sentenced to die, and thus unconditionally consecrated, can be redeemed; he must be put to death."

—Leviticus 27:29

Condemned murderers, idolaters, and clean animals marked for tithe (Ez. 20:37; Jer. 33:17) are cherem (*specially-devoted*), classified as kodesh kodashim (*especially holy*) to the LORD.

Proscribed property is specially devoted to God.

No monetary substitute is acceptable for cherem. A condemned person has no value [Rashi]. As with Canaanite property, things specially-devoted must be destroyed (Josh. 6:17; 7:1, 11-13, 15).

In contrast, firstfruits from the trees or from the land can be redeemed for the value assessed by the kohen plus 20% (Lev. 26:30-31). Tithed animals from the herd or flock are marked for dedication to the sanctuary (Jer. 31:14 (13תנ"ך); Ez. 20:37). The donor lines up the animals and indiscriminately marks every tenth animal. Marked animals cannot be exchanged. As with humans, those under cherem (*specially-devoted*) cannot be redeemed!

? ***Jeremiah 2:11 says, ". . . my people have exchanged their Glory for something without value." Explain Lev. 26:41-45 in light of Yisra'el's idolatry. Read Rev. 14:1, 4, 20:4. Are these marked men a tithe? Explain.***

Concluding Statement

> *“These are the mitzvot which Adonai gave to Moshe for the people of Isra’el on Mount Sinai.”*
> —*Leviticus 27:34*

This chapter concludes with mitzvot (*commandments*) for those who obligate themselves by making vows [Hirsch, p.510]. Its focus upon mitzvot contrasts with the “laws, rulings, and teachings” in a statement concluding the previous chapter: “These are the laws, rulings, and teachings that Adonai himself gave to the people of Isra’el on Mount Sinai through Moshe” (Lev. 26:46).

Commentators observe that attention to oaths and devoted objects in chapter 27 ties up loose ends, following the grand finale which links K’doshim (*holy ones*) with those who walk B’Chukotai (*in My statutes*).

Ascend in holiness to the place where God dwells.

Cherem denotes things *segregated by oath* and raised to a higher level of dedication than hekdesh (*ordinary consecration*) [Munk, p. 336]. Yirm’yahu (*Jeremiah*) calls Yisra’el holy (Jer. 2:3). Thus, Yisra’el can never be subject to substitution or replacement by another nation.

? *Read Ps. 132:2-5. Explain whether or not David found the place which he vowed, upon oath, to find, “a place for Adonai, a dwelling for the Mighty One of Ya’akov.” What makes Y’rushalayim a holy place to Yisra’el?*

Witness to the Nations *Meander*

"Heal me, ADONAI, and I will be healed; save me, and I will be saved, for you are my praise."
—Jeremiah 17:14

Intercede for your people! God burdens Yirm'yahu (*Jeremiah*) with a message of judgment and forbids him to marry or attend weddings (Jer. 16:1-2, 8-9). For this, his culture brands him a pariah and an object of social disgrace.

Loss of heritage can result from unatoned sin.

Yirm'yahu sees the day that nations will confess idolatry and turn to God (Jer. 16:19; cf. Dt. 32:21).

The prophet indicts Y'hudah (*Judah*) for hardheartedness. He uses a diamond-point to etch the accusation on the tablets of Y'hudah's heart (Jer. 17:1). Disaster strikes! For unatoned sin, says God, "I will cause you to serve your enemies." Y'hudah will lose its heritage—its land!

Those who forsake God are without help (cf. Mt. 22:11-14). Covenant breakers will be "put to shame," i.e. condemned [Thompson, p. 424n]. Yet all is not lost. The prophet turns to God for healing!

? *Read Proverbs 3:3, 7:3. Contrast the results of writing sin on the tablets of the heart (Jer. 17:1) with the results of writing covenant kindness and truth (chesed ve'emet) on the tablets of the heart.*

Election

" . . . for many are invited, but few are chosen. "
—Matthew 22:14

Matthew aims three parables in a row to describe the change of leadership over God's kingdom (Mt. 21:28-32, 33-46; 22:1-14). Of course, leadership has already passed from firstborns to the Levites and elders.

Leadership passes from the firstborns and Levites to the elect who are fruitful.

Now, it passes to those who are invited and elect to come, properly dressed, to the wedding banquet given by the king for his son (Mt. 22:2,11).

In ancient days, formal festivities required an advance invitation, followed by a second notification after the feast was prepared (Mt. 22:3-4, 8; note also, Esth. 5:, 6:14). The insult to the king is especially grave, since the food is ready and this is the second invitation!

In his anger, the king destroys those who have persecuted his servants and burns the city. Then he goes outside the city to invite wayfarers (Jew or gentile), to fill the room full (Mt. 22:9). The elect respond—on short notice!

***?** Read Judges 14:17. Wedding festivities could run for seven days. Sukkot, also a seven day festival, consummates God's rule over the nations. Read Zechariah 14:16-21. Relate Matthew's parable to the fulfillment of Sukkot.*

Talk Your Walk . . .

Walking in covenant relationship with God can never end for Yisra'el, because God remains ever faithful to His end of the agreement. Should Yisra'el choose to walk B'CHUKOTAI (*in My statutes*), then God promises fruitfulness, prosperity, and blessing for Yisra'el in the Land. Moreover, God will protect Yisra'el from her enemies and Yisra'el will rest with Him in the Land.

However, if Yisra'el chooses not to walk B'CHUKOTAI, then God will slowly withdraw His Presence and His protection from the camp. Spiritually, Yisra'el will walk a path toward Egypt. Starting with indentured servanthood, the path spirals into slavery to foreigners in foreign lands and even serving foreign idols!

Keeping Shabbats and Sh'mittah (*release* on sabbatical year) is particularly important. God puts Yisra'el in the Land to rest with Him, just as He once put Adam in Gan Eden to rest with Him. Yisra'el's failure to keep Shabbats holy diminishes the blessing of the triple harvest promised in year six. This, in turn, makes Sh'mittah too difficult to observe, afflicting the Land and leading to captivity. Then the Land, "desolate" of its people, can rest; whereas, the people are devoured in the land of their enemies until the Promised Land is repaid her lost Sabbaticals!

Rest in prosperity or be exiled for disobedience.

Oasis

. . . Walk Your Talk

God will "cause" us to walk upright and erect! Can greater blessing abound in life's journey than to "walk with God" with our heads held high? Surely this calling is reserved for the millennium, and yet this very same dream is available right now! Come to think of it, how can we expect to be completely prepared for Messiah's return if we're not completing our preparations at this time?

Some may think that Sabbatical rest is reserved for those who live in the Land. Others may think that Sh'mittah does not apply today, because the twelve tribes no longer exist and hereditary portions in the Land have ended. Some may think that Sh'mittah cannot be kept until a majority of Jews have returned to the Land. Still others may think the promises are corporate, not to be observed by individuals.

Yet clearly, God calls all believers everywhere to rest with Him. Keeping Shabbat holy acquires its own gravity. As Shabbat can sanctify the week, so Sh'mittah can sanctify the years. Only through faith will blessings abound for those who walk B'CHUKOTAI. Will *you* be blessed?

Walk in faith, and rest in the statutes!

Shabbat Shalom!

Yeshua tells the following story: "A certain creditor had two debtors; the one owed ten times as much as the other. When they were unable to pay him back, he canceled both their debts. Now which of them will love him more?" (Lk. 7:41-42).

Remember, God Himself has redeemed us from slavery in Egypt. We owe Him our lives! How much *more* do we owe Him our love? Yet human nature forgets; instead we ask, "What have you done for me lately?" We find ourselves in no mood to love God with wholeness of heart. We forget what God has done for our fathers!

We must approach God in holiness.

The covenant calls us to remember that He is our God and we are His people. We must transmit this heritage from Sinai to our children. VAYIKRA ADONAI (*and the LORD called*) to Moshe and the nation from within the Ohel Mo'ed (*Tent of Meeting*), to radiate holiness as a kingdom of priests and a holy nation.

Apart from Torah, one's understanding of holiness is subjective. God has taught us to maintain purity so that He will dwell among us. He promised to protect us with His Presence, if we would keep ourselves pure and keep His camp holy. He has instructed us to walk the paths of covenant blessing, and He has taught us to enter His Presence with sacrifice. But always, God teaches us to approach Him *His* way, not *our* way.

End

Ascending to approach God their own way costs Nadav and Avihu their lives! Ironically, these priestly sons ascend Mt. Sinai higher than anyone else, except for Moshe, Aharon, and Y'hoshua. But trying to enter the holiest place where God dwells, by making their own incense cloud with their own fire, fails to keep them pure enough to enter the Presence of God. They become their own offering—a holocaust. Afterward, God tells their father Aharon, "I will be glorified!"

Always remember the concluding blessing of the covenant cycle: va'olech etchem kom'miyut (*and I will cause you to walk with heads held high*)! God purposes to free us from slavery and the low self-esteem of serving as resident aliens in another's house!

Can you accept that God will structure life so you can walk with your head held high? Abide in His Presence, letting scripture and prayer inform your decisions. Balance your life in this world with the holiness that radiates from living in the Presence of God. Following God *His way* guarantees that you will hold your head high as you walk life's journey with Him. Chazak, chazak, v'nitchazek (*be strong, be strong, and may we be strengthened*)!!!

Let us walk with heads held high!

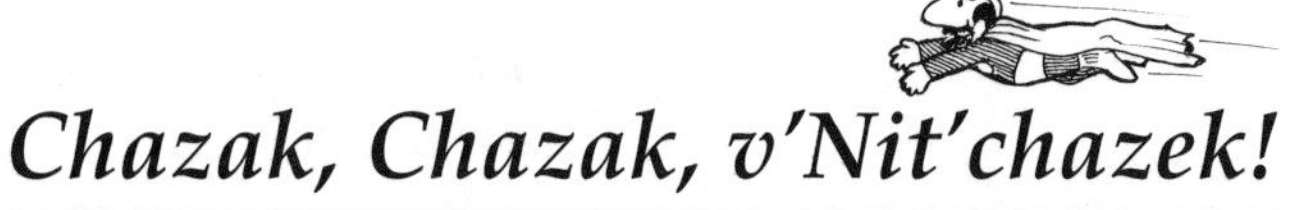

Chazak, Chazak, v'Nit'chazek!

Our rest stop ends
atop Sinai,
so pack your tent
and say goodbye.
But the beat goes on—
let the Torah roll
on to Numbers, Deuteronomy,
yes, the rest of the scroll.
At the end of each book,
we take a break.
Chazak, Chazak, v'Nit'chazek!

חזק חזק ונתחזק

Be strong, be strong,
and may we be strengthened!!!

Glossary

Pronunciation Tips

Place the emphasis on the syllable with the **bold** *print. In general, pronounce the vowels as follows:*

a—ah
e—ay or eh
i—ee
o—oh
u—oo

Wherever an apostrophe (') appears, pause briefly before beginning the next syllable. The symbol is used here to represent a schwa or a silent letter such as alef or ayin.

"Ch" is used to represent the sound of the letter chet or chaf. Pronounce it as in the name "Bach"—never as in "chew."

ACHAREI **MOT** (*after the death*)
achu**zah** (*land holding*)
ADONAI (*the* LORD)
afesis (Greek word meaning *removal of sins, release*)
Aha**ron** (*Aaron*)
alef (*first letter, Heb. alefbet*)
ali**yah** (*go up*)
Am ha**A**retz (*the people of the Land*)
Am Yisra'el **chai** (*the people of Israel live*)
Ani ADONAI m'kadish'**chem** (*I am the* LORD *Who-sanctifies-you*)
a**sham** (*reparation, guilt offering*)
a**sham** ta**lu**'i (*the doubtful reparation offering*)
Avi**hu** (*Abihu*)
avo**dah** (*work, servile labor, service, worship*)
azka**rah** (*reminder, memorial-portion*)
ba'al **ke**ri (*male with seminal emission*)
ba-**yom** ha-SH'MINI (*on the eighth day*)
B'CHUKOTAI (*in My statutes*)
beit ha-cha**tser** (*village house*)
beit mo**shav** (*residential house*)
B'HAR (*on the Mount*)
B'**HAR** **Sinai** (*on Mount Sinai*)
Bir**chat** Koha**nim** (*Aaronic Benediction*)
b'**nei** Yisra'**el** (*the children of Israel*)
BO (*enter!*)
B'REISHEET (*in the beginning*)
B'**rit** Chada**shah** (*New Covenant*/New Testament)
B'SHALACH (*when he let go*)
Cham (*Ham*)
Chanam'**el** (*Favor of God*)
chat**ta**'t (*sin offering, purification*)
CHAYEI SARAH (*the life of Sarah*)
Cha**zak**, cha**zak**, v'nitcha**zek**

(*Be strong, be strong, and may we be strengthened*)!!!
cha**zeh** (*breast*)
cherem (*set apart, restricted, specially-devoted, segregated by oath*)
chol (*common*)
chu**kim** (*statutes*)
C'**na**'an (*Canaan*)
cohen/cohanim—see kohen
dam sha**fach** (*shedder of blood*)
d'mei**hem** bam (*their blood is on them*)
d'**ror** (*liberty*)
egel (*calf, young bull*)
eker (*offshoot*)
El'a**zar** (*Eleazer*)
Eltsa**fan** (*Elzaphan*)
EMOR (*say!*)
eyl ha-milu**im** (*ram of ordination/filling of hands*)
ga**ba**chat (*forehead;* when applied to cloth, the *outside*)
Gan **E**den (*the Garden of Eden/Paradise*)
g'do**lah** (*major*)
ge**ma**tria (*calculation of numerical value of Hebrew words to search for hidden meanings; note Rev. 13:18*)
ger (*sojourner, resident alien*)
ge**rim** v'tosha**vim** (*sojourners and resident-settlers*)
ger to**shav** (*resident-settler*)
go**yim** (*gentiles, nations*)
g'**ris** (*large bean*)
g'**ulat olam** (*redemption right for the ages*)
Hafta**rah** (*conclusion*/ Prophets and Writings)
Hala**chah**/Hala**khah** (*Hebrew Law*)
hek**desh** (*ordinary consecration*)
Hevel (*Abel*)
Hithalach**ti** b'**toch'chem** (*I will walk about in your midst*),
isheh (*fire offering*)
issa**ron** (*one-tenth* ephah of flour; also called an "omer," a day's provision of flour, or two quarts)
Ita**mar** (*Ithamar*)
ka'**asher tsivah** ADONAI et **Moshe** (*exactly as the LORD commanded Moshe*)
ka**dosh** (*holy*)
Kappa**rah** (*atonement, covering*)
ka**ra**chat (*baldspot;* when applied to cloth, the *inside*)
ka**ret** (*cutting off, cutting short*)
kash**rut** (*kosher laws*)
K'DO**SHIM** (*holy ones*)
k'du**shah** (*a state of holiness*)
kip**per** (*atone for, expiate, purge*)
KI TISA (*when you elevate*)
koda**shim** (*holy (pl.); sacred offerings*)
kodesh (*holy*)
kodesh hilu**lim** l'ADONAI (*holy of praise to ADONAI*)

kodesh koda**shim** (*Holy of Holies; especially holy offerings*)
kod**shei** do**rot** (*permanent sacrifices,* lit. *holy things of the generations*)
kod**shei** koda**shim** (*most holy*)
kod**shei** sha'**ah** (*holy of moment,* i.e. *one-time sacrifice*)
koha**nim**/coha**nim** (*priests*)
ko**hen**/co**hen** (*priest*)
Kohen Ga**dol** (*High Priest*)
kol a**dat** Yisra'**el** (*the whole community of Israel*)
kom'mi**yut** (*and I shall cause you to walk upright*) (Lev. 26:12,13)
kor**ban** **oleh** v'yo**red** (near-offering, up and down)
kosher (Ashkenazi)/ka**sher** (Sephardic) (*fit, fit for eating*)
k'ta**nah** (*minor*)
LECH L'**CHA** (*go forth, yourself!*)
l'ga**lot** er**vah** (*to uncover nakedness*)
l'kid**desh** o**toh** (*to sanctify it, to declare it holy*)
ma'a**lah** ma'**al** (*breach of faith*)
macha**neh** sh'chi**nah** (*camp of the Glory*)
maf**tir** (*concluding*)
mam**le**chet koha**nim** v'**goy** ka**dosh** (*kingdom of priests and a holy nation*)
Melchi-**Tse**dek (*Melchizedek*)
Mid**rash** (*inquiry, rabbinical commentary on the Bible*)
MI**K**ETZ (*at the end of*)
mi**kra**'ei **ko**desh (*proclaiming of holiness*)
mik**veh** (*a body of living water*)
min**chah** (*grain offering, tribute, meal offering*)
min**chat** bikku**rim** (tribute of first-processed)
min**yan** (lit. *number/quorum of 10 adults for public prayer*)
Mir**yam** (*Miriam*)
Misha'**el** (*Mishael*)
mish**kan** (*tabernacle/God's dwelling*)
Mish**nah** (*teachings, the Oral Law compiled in 220 CE)*
MISHPA**TIM** (*judgments, ordinances*)
mi**tah** bi**dei** sha**ma**yim (*death by the hand of heaven*)
Mitz**ra**yim (*Egypt*)
mitz**vot** (*commands, commandments*)
m'kadish'**chem** (*the one-who-hallows you!*)
m'lach'**ah** (*assigned tasks, work*)
m'**le**chet avo**dah** (*servile work*)
M'na**sheh** (*Manasseh*)
mo'**ed** (*appointed time*)
Moshe (*Moses*)
M'TSO**RA** (*infected one*)
Na'a**man** (*Naaman*)

Na**dav** (*Nadab*)
na**si** (*leader*)
na**ta**ti SHA**LOM** (*I will give peace*) . . . v'hiSH**BAT**i cha**yah** (*and I will cause-to-cease wild beasts*)
Natzeret (*Nazereth*)
na**zir** (*consecrated, Nazirite*)
n'da**vah** (*free will, voluntary offering*)
neder (*vow, votive offerings*)
nefesh (*soul*)
nega (*affliction*)
nega tsa**ra**'at (*affliction of skin infection*)
netek (*scall*)
nid**dah** (*menstruation, menstruant,* lit. *separated*)
NOACH (*Noah/rest*)
n'vei**lah** (*died, not ritually slaughtered*)
Ohel Mo'**ed** (*Tent of Meeting*)
o**lah** (*ascent offering; burnt* or *whole offering*)
o**lat** ta**mid** (*daily/regular ascent offering*)
ona**nim** (*mourners,* pl.)
o**nen** (*mourner*)
or**lah** (*uncircumcision*)
pa**der** (*suet, fat*)
para**shah** (Torah *portion*)
parashi**ot** (Torah *portions,* pl.)
Pesach (*Passover*)
pid**yon** ha-**ben** (*redemption of the* firstborn *son*)
P'KU**DEI** (*accountings of*)
por**nei**a (Greek, *illicit sex*)
P'ru**shim** (*Pharisees*)
Rav (*Rabbi/Great One*)
Rav Sha'**ul** (*Paul*)
reiach ni**cho**ach (*a sweet savor*)
ri**shon** (*first*)
Rosh haSha**nah** (*the Head of the Year*)
Ruach ha**Ko**desh (*Holy Spirit*)
r'vi'**i** (*fourth*)
S'**dom** (*Sodom*)
seder (lit. *order*, a ritual meal eaten in a specific order to commemorate the Passover story)
SEFER B'**R**EI**SHEET** *(Book of Genesis/in the beginning)*
SEFER SH'**MOT** *(Book of Exodus/names)*
SEFER VA**Y**I**KRA** (*Book of Leviticus/then He called*)
Shab**bat** (*Sabbath*)
Sha'**ul** (*Saul / Paul*)
shavtah la'**a**retz (*Sabbath-ceasing for the Land*)
Shavu'**ot** (lit. *weeks*, Feast of Weeks, Pentecost)
she**ni** (*second*)
sh'**er** (*close family, flesh relation;* plural sh'**erim**)
shi**shi** (*sixth*)
sh'la**mim** (*sacrifice of fellowship/wholeness/well-being;* often called a *peace offering*)
shli**shi** (*third*)

Sh'mini (*eighth*)
Sh'**mi**ni At**se**ret (*"eighth termination,"* last convocation day of the Torah, celebrated at the end of Sukkot)
Sh'mit**tah** (*release* on sabbatical year)
Sh'mot (*names/Exodus*)
sh'va**rim**-t'ru'**ah** (*broken-wailing*, two broken sounds of the shofar; following the long, unbroken t'ki'**ah**)
shvi'**i** (*seventh*)
Si**fra** (Aramaic, *"The Book,"* an early Halachic Midrash (commentary) on Leviticus)
Sim**chat** To**rah** (*joy of the Torah*)
si**nat** chi**nam** (*hatred for one's fellow man*)
s'mi**chah** (*laying on of hands*)
solet (*semolina*)
Suk**kot** (*Succoth, huts, booths*)
ta**hor** (*ritually pure/not impure, undefiled, not contagious*)
taho**rah** (*a state of purity*)
talmi**dim** (*students/disciples*)
Tal**mud** (*commentary on the Mishnah*)
tam (*whole, perfect, pure, perfection, unblemished*)
tam'**ah** (*ritually impure,* fem. form; see ta**mei**)
ta**mei** (*ritually impure/contagious/defiled*; fem. tam'**ah**; pl. tam'**u**)
"Ta**mei**! Ta**mei**! (*Defiled! Defiled!*)
ta**mid** (*daily offering*)
tam'**u** (*ritually impure*, pl. form; see ta**mei**)
Ta**nakh** (תנ"ך, *an acronym for the Hebrew canon; **T**orah, **N**'vi'im/Prophets, and **K**'tuvim/Writings*)
Tazria (*she bears seed*)
Tetra**gram**maton, יהוה (*Yod-Hay-Vav-Hay; the four-letter name of Adonai*)
tira'u (*must hold in awe*)
tit'**ha**ru (*you shall become pure*)
t'nu**fah** (*elevation offering*)
to**dah** (*thanksgiving, thank offering*)
to'**evah** (*abomination*)
Tol'dot (*generations, life story, offspring*)
tor (*turtledove*)
To**rah** (*instruction*/Pentateuch, Gen.-Dt.)
to**rat** (*instruction of*)
to**shav** (*settler*)
t'rei**fah** (*torn*)
T'rumah (*offering*)
tsa**ra**'at (*contagious skin infection,* scaly *skin disease,* sometimes translated *leprosy* from the Greek word lepra)
Tsav (*command!*)
T'tsaveh (*you shall command*)
tum'**ah** (*contaminated*)

unkosher (*not fit* for a priestly people to eat)
va'o**lech** et**chem** kom'mi**yut** (*and I will* <u>*cause*</u> *you to walk with heads held high*)!
VAERA (*and I appeared*)
VAYAKHEL (*and he assembled*)
VAY'CHI (*and he lived*)
VAYERA (*and He appeared*)
VA**Y**ESHEV (*and he settled*)
VAYETSE (*and he went out*)
VAYIGASH (*and he drew near*)
VAYIKRA (*and He called/ Leviticus*)
VAYIKRA ADONAI (*and the LORD called*)
VAYIKRA ADONAI el Mo**she** (*and the LORD called to Moses*)
VAYISHLACH (*and he sent*)
vi**dui** (*confession*)
Y'chez**kel** (*Ezekiel*)
Yefet (*Japheth*)
Ye**shu**a (*Jesus/salvation*)
Ye**shu**a haMa**shi**ach (*Jesus the Messiah*)
Y'hu**dah** (*Judah*)
Yirm'**ya**hu (*Jeremiah*)
Yisra'**el** (*Israel*)
YITRO (*Jethro/abundance*)
Yocha**nan** (*John*)
Yom haKippu**rim** (*the day of atonements*)
Yom Kip**pur** (*Day of Atonement*)
Yom T'ru**ah** (*the day of horn-blasting*/also *Rosh haShanah*)
Yo**vel** (*Jubilee, Homebringing*)
Y'rusha**la**yim (*Jerusalem*)
zav (*one suffering from a discharge*)
zav she**ni** (*zav, second time*)
za**vah** (*one-with-a-flow; one who discharges on days other than menstruation*; fem. form of *zav*)
za**vah** g'do**lah** (lit. *big flow*; three flows in three successive days)
Z'char**yah** (*Zechariah*)
zevach sh'la**mim** (*sacrifice of fellowship / wholeness/well-being*; often called a *peace offering*)
zeva**chim** (*slaughter-offerings*)
zi**chron** t'ru'**ah** (*a reminder by horn-blasting*)
יהוה (See *Tetragrammaton*.)
תנ"ך (Hebrew verse numbers occasionally vary from the English references. In this case, the Hebrew references are indicated by this symbol. For an explanation, see *Tanakh*.)

Bibliography

Alcalay, Reuben. *The Complete English-Hebrew, Hebrew-English Dictionary*. Ramat Gan: Massadah Publishing Co., 1981.

Alter, Robert. *The Art of Biblical Narrative.* Berkeley, CA: Basic Books, 1981.

Alter, Robert. *Leviticus: Translation and Commentary.* First edition. New York: W. W. Norton & Company, 1996.

Ant., Antiq., see The Antiquities of the Jews in *The Works of Josephus.*

Attridge, Harold W. *The Epistle to the Hebrews.* In Helmut Koester (Gen. Ed.), *Hermeneia.* Philadelphia: Fortress Press, 1989.

Averbeck, Richard E. Mikdash, in W. A.VanGemeren (Gen. Ed.), *New International Dictionary of Old Testament Theology and Exegesis* (Volume 2, pp. 1078-1087). Grand Rapids, MI: Zondervan Publishing House, 1997.

Avot, Pirkei Avot, see *The Metsudah Pirkei Avos: The Wisdom of the Fathers.*

Bava Kamma, see Schorr, *Talmud Bavli.*

Bav. Metzia, see Schorr, *Talmud Bavli.*

Ben-Abba, Dov. *Signet Hebrew-English English-Hebrew Dictionary.* Massada-Press/Modan Publishing House Ltd., Israel, 1977.

Ben Avraham, Rabbi Alexander, and Sharfman, Rabbi Benjamin (Eds.). *The Pentateuch and Rashi s Commentary.* Brooklyn, NY: S. S. & R. Publishing Company, Inc. (also Philadelphia: Press of the Jewish Publication Society), 1976.

Birnbaum, Philip. *Encyclopedia of Jewish Concepts.* NY: Hebrew Publishing Company, 1993.

Birnbaum, Philip (Ed.). *Maimonides Mishneh Torah.* New York: Hebrew Publishing Co., 1985.

Blackman, Philip (Ed.). *Mishnayoth.* Gateshead: Judaica Press, Ltd., 1983.

Bock, Darrell. L. *Luke.* In Moises Silva (Gen. Ed.), *Baker Exegeti-*

cal Commentary on the New Testament. Two volumes. Grand Rapids, MI: Baker Book House, 1994.

Bruce, F. F. *The Epistle to the Hebrews*. In F. F. Bruce (Gen. Ed.), *The New International Commentary on the New Testament*. Grand Rapids, MI: Wm. B. Eerdmans Publishing Company, 1979.

Bullinger, E. W. *Figures of Speech Used in the Bible*. Grand Rapids, MI: Baker Book House, 1987. (Original work published in 1898).

Carson, D. A. *Exegetical Fallacies*. Grand Rapids, MI, Baker Book House, 1984.

Carson, D.A. *Matthew*. In F. E. Gaebelien (Gen. Ed.), *The Expositor s Bible Commentary*. Volume 8. Grand Rapids, MI: Zondervan, 1984.

Childs, Brevard S. *Biblical Theology of the Old and New Testaments: Theological Reflection on the Christian Bible*. Minneapolis: Fortress Press, 1993.

Cohen, A. (Gen. Ed.). *Soncino Books of the Bible*. Volumes 1-14. London: The Soncino Press Limited, 1978.

Concordance to the Novum Testamentum Graece. Third edition. Berlin: Walter De Gruyter, 1987.

Douglas, Mary. *Leviticus as Literature*. Oxford: Oxford University Press, 1999.

Drazin, Israel. *Targum Onkelos to Leviticus: an English Translation of the Text with Analysis and Commentary* (Based on the A. Sperber and A. Berliner Editions). University of Denver: Center for Judaic Studies, 1994.

Driver, S. R., Plummer, A., and Briggs, C. A. (Gen. Eds.). *The International Critical Commentary on the Holy Scriptures of the Old and New Testaments*. Edinburgh: T. & T. Clark, 1979. (Original work published 1896-1924).

Ellingworth, Paul. *The Epistle to the Hebrews*. In I. Howard Marshall and W. Ward Gasque (Gen. Eds.), *The New International Greek New Testament Commentary*. Grand Rapids, MI: William B. Eerdmans Publishing Company, 1993.

Elwell, W. A. (Ed.). *Evangelical Dictionary of Theology.* Grand Rapids, MI: Baker Book House, 1984.

Evans, Louis H., Jr. *Hebrews.* In Lloyd J. Ogilvie (Gen. Ed.), *The Communicator s Commentary.* Dallas: Word Publishing, 1985.

Even-Shoshan, Avraham (Ed.). *New Concordance for the Torah, Prophets, and Writings.* Jerusalem: Sivan Press, 1977.

Feinberg, Jeffrey Enoch. *Walk Genesis!* Baltimore: Messianic Jewish Publishers, 1998.

Feinberg, Jeffrey Enoch. *Walk Exodus!* Baltimore: Messianic Jewish Publishers, 1999.

Fisch, S. *Ezekiel.* In A. Cohen (Gen. Ed.), *The Soncino Books of the Bible.* Volume 7. London: The Soncino Press, Ltd., 1978.

Fox, Everett. *The Schocken Bible: The Five Books of Moses.* Volume 1. New York: Schocken Books, 1995.

Frankel, Ellen and Teutsch, Betsy P. (1992). *The Encyclopedia of Jewish Symbols.* Northvale, NJ: Jason Aronson, 1992.

Friedman, Rabbi Alexander Zusia. *Wellsprings of Torah.* Transl. by Gertrude Hirschler. New York: Judaica Press, Inc., 1990.

Gerstenberger, Erhard S. *Leviticus: a Commentary.* The Old Testament Library. Louisville: Westminster John Knox Press, 1996.

Ginzberg, Louis. *The Legends of the Jews.* Volume 2. Transl. by Henrietta Szold. Baltimore: The Johns Hopkins University Press, 1998.

Gordon, Cyrus H. *Before the Bible.* New York: Harper and Row, 1962.

Gorman, Frank H., Jr. *Leviticus: Divine Presence in Community.* In George A. F. Knight and Frederick Carlson Holmgren (Gen. Eds.), *International Theological Commentary.* Grand Rapids, MI: William B. Eerdmans Publishing Company, 1997.

Gundry, Robert H. *Matthew: A Commentary on his Literary and Theological Art.* Grand Rapids, MI: Wm. B. Eerdmans Publishing Company, 1982.

Hartley, John E. *Leviticus.* In David A. Hubbard and Glenn W. Barker (Gen. Eds.), *Word Biblical Commentary.* Volume 4. Dallas: Word Books, Publisher, 1992.

Herczeg, Rabbi Yisrael Isser Zvi (Ed.). *The Torah: With Rashi s Commentary Translated, Annotated, and Elucidated.* Artscroll Series/The Sapirstein Edition. Brooklyn: Mesorah Publications, Ltd., 1995.

Hertz, Dr. J. H. (Ed.). *The Pentateuch and Haftorahs.* Second edition. London: Soncino Press, 1975.

Hilton, Rabbi Michael and Marshall, Fr. Gordion. *The Gospels & Rabbinic Judaism: A Study Guide*. Hoboken, NJ: KTAV, 1988.

Hirsch, Samson Raphael, Trans. *The Pentateuch, Haftarah, and the Five Megillot*. Ed. by Ephraim Oratz. New York: The Judaica Press, Inc., 1990. (English translation by Gertrude Hirschler; German work published in 1867-1878).

Ibn Ezra, see Schorr, *Talmud Bavli.*

ibn Paquda, R. Bachya. *Duties of the Heart.* Transl. by Moses Hyamson. Jerusalem: Feldheim Publishers, 1986. (Translated from Arabic into Hebrew by R. Yehuda Ibn Tibbon).

Joosten, Jan. *People and Land in the Holiness Code: An Exegetical Study of the Ideational Framework of the Law in Leviticus 17-26.* Leiden: E.J. Brill, 1996.

Kahan, Rabbi Aharon. *The Taryag Mitzvos.* Brooklyn: Keser Torah Pub., 1988. (Based on the classical *Sefer haChinuch*).

Kantor, Mattis. *The Jewish Time Line Encyclopedia: A Year-by-Year History from Creation to the Present.* Northvale, NJ: Jason Aronson, Inc., 1989.

Keil, C. F. and Delitzsch, F. *Commentary on the Old Testament.* Transl. by James Martin. Volumes 1-10. Grand Rapids, MI: William B. Eerdmans Publishing Company, 1976.

Kent, Homer A. *The Epistle to the Hebrews.* Grand Rapids, MI: Baker Book House, 1985.

Ker., Kereisos, see Schorr, *Talmud Bavli.*

Kidd., Kiddushin, see Schorr, *Talmud Bavli.*

Kohlenberger, John R. III (Ed.). *The NIV Interlinear Hebrew-English Old Testament.* Grand Rapids, MI: Zondervan Publishing House, 1979.

Kolatch, Alfred J. *The Complete Dictionary of English and Hebrew*

First Names. Middle Village, NY: Jonathan David Publishers, Inc., 1984.

Lachs, Samuel Tobias. *A Rabbinic Commentary on the New Testament.* Hoboken, NJ: KTAV Publishing House, Inc., 1987.

Lane, William L. *Hebrews: A Call to Commitment.* Peabody, MA: Hendrickson Publishers, 1988.

Lane, William L. *Word Biblical Commentary: Hebrews 1-13.* Volumes 47a, 47b. Waco, TX: Word Books, Publisher, 1991.

Leibowitz, Nehama. *Studies in Bereshit (Leviticus).* Transl. by Aryeh Newman. Fourth revised edition. Jerusalem: Hemed Press, 1994.

Levine, Baruch A. *Leviticus.* In Nahum M. Sarna (Gen. Ed.), *The JPS Torah Commentary.* Philadelphia: The Jewish Publication Society, 1989.

Lev. R., Leviticus Rabbah, see *Soncino Midrash Rabbah.*

Men., Menachot, see Schorr, *Talmud Bavli.*

The Metsudah Pirkei Avos: The Wisdom of the Fathers. Selected and translated by Rabbi Avrohom Davis. New York: Metsudah Publications, 1986.

Michaels, J. Ramsey. *1 Peter.* In David A. Hubbard and Glenn W. Barker (Gen. Eds.), *Word Biblical Commentary.* Volume 49. Waco, TX: Word Books, Publisher, 1988.

Midrash Tanchuma. See Townsend, John T.

Milgrom, Jacob. *Leviticus 1-16.* The Anchor Bible. NY: Doubleday, a division of Random House, 1991.

Milgrom, Jacob. *Leviticus 17-22.* The Anchor Bible. NY: Doubleday, a division of Random House, 2000.

Mishnah [Yoma 3-7], see Phillip Blackman (Ed.), *Mishnayot.*

M. Neg., Mishnah Negaim, see Phillip Blackman (Ed.), *Mishnayot.*

Munk, Rabbi Elie. *The Call of the Torah: An Anthology of Interpretation and Commentary on the Five Books of Moses: VAYIKRA.* Translated from the French by E. S. Maser. In R. Nosson Scherman and R. Meir Zlotowitz (Eds.), *ArtScroll Mesiorah Series.* Brooklyn, NY: Mesorah Publications, Ltd., 1992.

M. Zev., Mishnah Zevachim, see Phillip Blackman (Ed.), *Mishnayot*.

Nachshoni, Yehuda. *Studies in the Weekly Parashah*. Transl. by Shmuel Himelstein. Volume 3. Brooklyn: Mesorah Publications, Ltd., 1989.

Ned., Nedarim, see Schorr, *Talmud Bavli.*

Neusner, Jacob. *Sifra: an Analytical Translation.* Brown Judaic Studies 138-140. Atlanta: Scholars Press, 1988

The New English Bible. Standard edition. New York: Oxford University Press, 1971.

Nidd., Niddoth, see Schorr, *Talmud Bavli.*

Novum Testamentum Graece. Nestle-Aland Edition. Stuttgart: Deutsche Bibelstiftung, 1981.

Num. R., Numbers Rabbah, see *Soncino Midrash Rabbah.*

Oppen, Menachem Moshe. *The Yom Kippur Avodah.* The Pictorial Avodah Series. Distributed by C.I. S. Distributors. Baltimore: M chon Harbotzas Torah, Inc. and Chicago: Chicago Community Kollel, 1988.

Pes., Pesachim, see Schorr, *Talmud Bavli.*

Plaut, W. Gunther. *The Haftarah Commentary*. Transl. by Chaim Stern. New York: UAHC Press, 1996.

Rambam, see Birnbaum, *Maimonides Mishneh Torah.*

Ramban (Nachmanides), Commentary on the Torah: Sefer vaYikra. Transl. by Rabbi Dr. Charles B. Chavel. NY: Shilo Publishing House, 1974.

Rashbam, see Schorr, *Talmud Bavli*.

Rashi. See Ben Avraham, Rabbi Abraham et al. or Herczek, Rabbi Yisrael Isser Zvi.

R.H., Rosh HaShannah, see Schorr, *Talmud Bavli.*

Robertson, A. T. *Word Pictures in the New Testament.* Grand Rapids, MI: Baker Book House, 1932.

Sailhamer, John H. *The Expositor s Bible Commentary: Leviticus.* Volume 2. Grand Rapids, MI: Zondervan Publishing House, 1990.

Sailhamer, John H. (1992). *The Pentateuch as Narrative*. Grand

Rapids, MI: Zondervan Publishing House, 1992.
Sawyer, John F. A. (Ed.). *Reading Leviticus: A Conversation with Mary Douglas.* In David J. A. Clines and Philip R. Davies (Gen. Eds.), *Journal for the Study of Old Testament.* Series 227. Sheffield, England: Sheffield Academic Press, 1996.
Scherman, Rabbi Nosson (Gen. Ed.). *The Chumash.* Ed. by Rabbi Hersh Goldwurn, Rabbi Avie Gold, and Rabbi Meir Zlotowitz. Artscroll Series, The Stone Edition. Brooklyn: Mesorah Publications, Ltd., 1995.
Schorr, Rabbi Yisroel Simcha (Gen. Ed.). *Talmud Bavli.* The Artscroll Series, Schottenstein Edition. Brooklyn: Mesorah Publications, Ltd., 1993.
Sforno, Ovadiah. *Commentary on the Torah.* Transl. by Rabbi Raphael Pelcovitz. The Artscroll Mesorah Series. Brooklyn: Mesorah Publications, Ltd., 1997.
Shabb., Shabbos, see Schorr, *Talmud Bavli.*
Shev., Shevuos, see Schorr, *Talmud Bavli.*
Shulman, Eliezer. *The Sequence of Events in the Old Testament.* Transl. by Sarah Lederhendler. Fifth edition. Jerusalem: Investment Co. of Bank Hapoalim and Ministry of Defense Publishing House, 1987.
Sifra. See Neusner, Jacob.
Skinner, John. *The International Critical Commentary: Leviticus.* Second edition. Edinburgh: T&T Clark Ltd., 1994.
Soncino, see A. Cohen (Ed.), *The Soncino Books of the Bible.*
Sot., Sotah, see Schorr, *Talmud Bavli.*
The Soncino Midrash Rabbah. The CD Rom Judaic Classics Library. Distributed by Davka Corporation. Brooklyn, NY: Soncino Press, 1983.
Speiser, E.A. *The Anchor Bible: Leviticus, A New Translation with Introduction and Commentary.* New York: Doubleday, 1962.
Stern, David H., Trans. *Complete Jewish Bible.* Clarksville, MD: Jewish New Testament Publications, 1998.
Stern, David H. *Jewish New Testament Commentary.* Clarksville, MD: Jewish New Testament Publications, 1992.

Sternberg, Meir. *The Poetics of Biblical Narrative*. Bloomington: Indiana University Press, 1987.
Stone Edition, see Scherman, Rabbi Nosson (Gen. Ed.).
Talmud, see Schorr, *Talmud Bavli.*
Targum Onkelos. See Drazin, Israel.
Tem., Temidim, see Philip Blackman (Ed.), *Mishnayoth.*
Tenney, Merrill C. *John.* Volume 9. Grand Rapids, MI: Zondervan Publishing House, 1981.
Tikkun Kor im haM fuar. Brooklyn, NY: Im haSefer, 1994.
Townsend, John T. *Midrash Tanhuma.* Translated into English with Indices and Brief Notes (S. Buber Recension). Hoboken, NY: KTAV Publishing House, 1997.
vaYikra R., see *Soncino Midrash Rabbah.*
Von Rad, Gerhard. *The Old Testament Library: Leviticus.* Revised edition. Philadelphia: The Westminster Press, 1972.
Walk Exodus, see Feinberg.
Wenham, Gordon J. *The Book of Leviticus.* In R. K. Harrison (Gen. Ed.), *The New International Commentary on the Old Testament.* Grand Rapids, MI: Wm B. Eerdmans Publ. Co., 1979.
Werblowsky, Dr. R. J. Zwi and Wigoder, Dr. Geoffrey (Eds.). *The Encyclopedia of the Jewish Religion.* Jerusalem: Masada, 1967.
Wigram, George V. *The Englishman s Hebrew and Chaldee Concordance of the Old Testament.* Grand Rapids, MI: Baker Book House, 1980. (Original work published in 1843).
Warning, Wilfried. *Literary Artistry in Leviticus.* In R. Alan Culpepper and Rolf Rendtorr (Eds.), *Biblical Interpretation Series.* Volume 35. Leiden: E.J. Brill, 1999.
The Works of Josephus. Transl. by William Whiston. Lynn, MA: Hendrickson Publishers, 1980.
Yoma, see Schorr, *Talmud Bavli.*
Zav., Zavim, see Blackman, *Mishnayoth.*
Zev., Zevachim, see Schorr, *Talmud Bavli.*
Zornberg, Avivah Gottlieb. *Leviticus: The Beginning of Desire.* Philadelphia: The Jewish Publication Society, 1995.